# MANAGER'S PUBLIC RELATIONS HANDBOOK

**Nathaniel N. Sperber**
Public Relations Consultant

**Otto Lerbinger**
Professor of Public Relations
Co-editor of *pr reporter*

**Addison-Wesley Publishing Company**
Reading, Massachusetts • Menlo Park, California
London • Amsterdam • Don Mills, Ontario • Sydney

**Library of Congress Cataloging in Publication Data**

Sperber, Nathaniel H.
  Manager's public relations handbook.

  Includes index.
  1. Public relations.  2. Industrial management.
I. Lerbinger, Otto.  II. Title.
HD59.S66      659.2′024658      81-22896
ISBN 0-201-14199-X           AACR2

Photographs on pages xi, 22, 34, 156, and 248 are courtesy of Fredrik D. Bodin.
Photographs on pages 128, 248, and 306 are courtesy of Pamela Price.
Photograph on page 180 is courtesy of Nancy Dudley.

Our thanks to the many people who helped make this handbook possible:

- ► Numerous public relations professionals who sent us their most useful checklists.
- ► Corporations, nonprofits, and government agencies that allowed us to examine their policies and materials.
- ► Richard Staron, senior business editor, who was of invaluable editorial assistance.
- ► Nancy Dudley, whose skills are evident in the photographic illustrations.
- ► Marilyn Wood, a speedy typist who kept us on schedule.

People do what is inspected, not expected.

Anonymous

# CONTENTS

# PREFACE

The effective manager excels in handling exceptional situations with perspective and dispatch. In today's turbulent society, a manager is judged by how well he or she responds to crises and critical issues. How quickly and adequately they are detected, analyzed, and resolved spells success or disaster for an organization. A manager is praised or reproached by superiors depending on his or her adroit handling of non-routine problems.

Major problems and uncertainties in the post-industrial society are largely of a public relations nature. Requirements, demands, and expectations of a wide variety of publics impinge on managers. Examples of some are:

> ► Government sets the framework within which private organizations operate. Regulations increasingly prescribe product standards, worker health and safety requirements, air and water pollution limits, financial disclosure requirements, etc.

▶ Consumer, environmental, and other social action groups—the so-called third sector—monitor business performance. Like labor unions before them, they make demands for a change in business practices.

▶ Employees seek quality of work-life as well as high wages and fringe benefits.

▶ Stockholders want reforms in corporate governance and cessation of socially harmful policies, e.g., doing business in South Africa.

▶ General public frown on greediness of corporations at the expense of the public interest.

To respond to these challenges, managers must apply public relations principles and skills. Public relations is not only a specialized occupation but a growing aspect of most top and middle management job descriptions. The reason is that the need by organizations to make adjustments with other groups in society has become more important.

This handbook is intended for both the general manager and the public relations professional. Both need to remember the myriad "things" that must be attended to or implemented to bring about success or to prevent failure in a variety of happenings or events. That is the function of a checklist. This handbook is the only known compilation of checklists for anticipating, handling, and following up events or crises.

A manager's use of a checklist can be likened to that of an airline pilot. Before any aircraft leaves the ground, the pilot—who may well be a veteran of 25 years of flight experience—conscientiously runs through an exhaustive checklist of instruments, linkages, wheels, hydraulics, servomechanisms, etc. He checks every single unit, for failure of any single item could mean disaster, and remembering to check everything could mean a safe flight.

The checklist he uses does not tell him how to take off. It does not instruct him how to land. It does not describe flight procedures. It is a tool used to ascertain that the pilot has overlooked nothing in his prevention of accident or has been reminded of every procedure to achieve a successful flight.

The chief executive of a corporation or the administrator of a hospital might be called upon to respond to a controversial charge on national TV. A company decides to close down an assembly plant, laying off hundreds of men and women. Another organization is faced with a consumer boycott of its principal product as a result of a governmental agency's edict.

In these cases, and scores of others just as disparate, the public relations practitioner, or the person responsible for the handling of a "happening," is confronted with the need to establish and implement procedures leading to a successful conclusion. It is then that he or she must remember all those entries in a pragmatic checklist.

This is not a public relations primer or handbook. It is not designed to "teach" public relations. It is a collection of fifty-six checklists, each of which has evolved as a result of numerous uses. Not every one will include every possible or unforeseeable item. Most of the usual and predictable entries are here.

In the use of any of the lists, any individual reader may find the need for modifications to accommodate special circumstances. Aside from these variables, this book will aid managers and practitioners to tailor lists and add others to fit their climates and conditions.

Use of checklists does not mean that managers react only to anticipate events and plan for them. They must also initiate actions intended to forestall events or to produce desired results.

Many checklists in this book will help a public relations practitioner to establish on-going communication systems and programs with key publics. Checklists on consumer participation, employee communications, training programs, community lines of communication, and annual and interim reports itemize the ingredients for effective links with an organization's stakeholders.

In addition to reacting to situations and planning for them, managers and public relations consultants can use these checklists to audit public relations programs and activities. For example, they can ascertain whether an organization has an effective feedback system with its customers, employees, and stockholders. They can determine whether its social responsibility programs conform to generally accepted guidelines.

Introductory explanations precede each section of this book and each checklist. Their purpose is to provide background, basic principles, and illustrations of applications. These introductions explain the rationale behind the checklists. By reading them, seasoned practitioners may be reminded of additional items to add to checklists as they are applied to specific situations. In fact, extra space is provided after each list for this purpose. Non-public relations professionals can treat these introductions as outlines of major ideas underlying public relations practice.

To use the lists, it is suggested that photocopies be made and given to each responsible person, together with assignments and time sequences, for each need.

Use of the handbook will create a greater awareness by management and staffs of the minutia concomitant with situations continually facing corporations, nonprofits, and other groups. Recognition and handling of the aggregation of these details spell the difference between success and failure of managers.

# CRISES

Quick action, peak performance, and ingenuity are demanded by crisis situations. Every public relations practitioner must be prepared to handle crises because at some time or another their employers or clients will face them. By definition, a crisis occurs infrequently and unpredictably. When it strikes, the public relations director and his or her team undergo the acid test. Personal strengths and shortcomings as well as the soundness of the public relations department structure are exposed.

Crises are of many kinds. A survey of Chief Executive Officers (CEOs) conducted by the authors showed that they treated proxy fights and acquisitions or tender offers as major crises. These strike at the heart of a CEO's personal survival. Condemnation by a governmental agency—FTC, FDA, SEC, etc.—was treated as a crisis by only 20 percent of them. Many others, however, would show "extreme concern." From a public relations viewpoint, both types of situations would have to be treated as crises.

Other kinds of crises are:

- ► Natural disasters—floods, tornadoes, earthquakes.
- ► Other actual disasters—fires, explosions, plane crashes.
- ► Litigation—product liability suits, minority stockholder suits for mismanagement.
- ► System breakdowns—power failures, gas shortages.

Management expects the public relations department to serve as a first line of defense in three respects:

**1.** Contain the damaging effects of the crisis on the company's reputation.

**2.** Provide an early warning system of crises caused by government or dissident groups.

**3.** Intervene in crises caused by human conflicts.

The loss of lives, and injury and damage caused by disasters is only the physical dimension. Another dimension is how opinions toward the company of important publics are affected. Is the company seen as poorly run? Are its products and services in question? Is it an unsafe place to work? Questions like these are on people's minds as the media automatically focus attention on the company. Low profile strategies don't work during a crisis. The company is on center stage and every step and utterance are watched. Public relations practitioners coordinate this public drama.

**CONFLICT RESOLUTION** When individuals and groups deliberately create crises to press demands on a company, public relations practitioners intervene. Media relations is only part of their function. The other is to use their communication and mediating skills in an attempt to resolve the conflict. Practitioners are usually more sensitive to currents of social change than general management and can serve to communicate new social expectations to top management. This societal feedback role of public relations is becoming increasingly recognized by management.

To signal impending crises with dissident groups and government bodies, public relations practitioners have set up socio-political monitoring systems. They keep track of emerging issues and the interest shown in them by activist groups and government. They also monitor legislative and administrative bodies and agencies for actions that might be taken relevant to the company.

This monitoring activity has become part of a larger public relations function which is often called issues management. Its purpose is precisely to avoid surprises by anticipating what may happen and, where possible, to intervene early enough in the build-up of a crisis to avert it.

# 1

# DISASTERS AND CATASTROPHES

When plane crashes, explosions, floods, tornadoes, and atomic power plant radiation leaks occur, normal management routines are disrupted and many managers and employees work under high stress conditions.

Public relations personnel are among the most affected. They must service the news media who are drawn to disasters, prevent the spread of rumors, and help restore order.

Although public relations is indeed cast in the reactive fire-fighting role, professionals prepare for the possibility or eventuality of a disaster by drafting contingency plans.

The following checklist outlines what to do when disaster strikes. Contingency plans try to anticipate each of these steps by making pre-decisions wherever possible.

| Disasters and Catastrophes | Assigned to | Date/Time Assigned | Date/Time Completed |
|---|---|---|---|
| I. Implement contingency plan. | _____ | _____ | _____ |
| II. Assign PR and "borrowed" personnel for each specific task. | _____ | _____ | _____ |
| III. Establish HQ (headquarters), field stations(s), and press rooms. | _____ | _____ | _____ |
|    1. Inform and clear with community leaders. | | | |
|    2. Inform and set up liaison with: | | | |
|       a. Police. | | | |
|       b. Same with fire department. | | | |
|       c. Red Cross and civilian defense. | | | |
|       d. Hospitals. | | | |
|       e. Federal agencies, e.g., FAA, CG, DOD. | | | |
| IV. Aggressively gather all information on nature of catastrophe, victims, survivors, damages, property damage, relationships, etc., and notify pertinent people. | _____ | _____ | _____ |
|    1. Assess impacts on ancillary people. | | | |
|    2. Cover and obtain essential factors for news points: | | | |
|       a. What happened? | | | |
|       b. How? | | | |
|       c. When? | | | |
|       d. Where? | | | |
|       e. Why? | | | |
|       f. Who and how many involved? | | | |
|       g. Ramifications: Physical? Financial? Locally? Nationally? Industry? | | | |
| V. Prepare news release/company statement. | _____ | _____ | _____ |
|    1. Include all known facts. | | | |

(continued)

| Disasters and Catastrophes | Assigned to | Date/Time Assigned | Date/Time Completed |
|---|---|---|---|
| 2. Be certain that all information is accurate. | | | |
| 3. Never release unconfirmed or speculative information. | | | |
| 4. Withhold names of victims until next-of-kin have been notified. | | | |
| VI. Clear statement/release with: | _____ | _____ | _____ |
| 1. Senior management. | | | |
| 2. Legal department. | | | |
| 3. Personnel department. | | | |
| 4. Union(s). | | | |
| 5. Police, fire, regulatory agencies, community leaders. | | | |
| VII. Obtain pertinent quote from CEO (designee) and insert in release. | _____ | _____ | _____ |
| VIII. Issue release immediately to: | _____ | _____ | _____ |
| 1. General-interest local and national electronic and print media. | | | |
| 2. Pertinent trade and industry publications. | | | |
| 3. Weeklies and monthlies. | | | |
| 4. Employees by bulletin boards and phone networks. | | | |
| 5. Community leaders. | | | |
| 6. Insurance company. | | | |
| 7. Pertinent governmental agencies. | | | |
| IX. Set up field press room(s) and the "Crisis Communication Center." (See Press Room Checklist.) | _____ | _____ | _____ |
| 1. Select site that is isolated from restricted areas and away from scene of immediate accident. | | | |
| 2. Notify news media of location of press room. | | | |
| 3. Arrange telephone lines and switch-ins from PR department to press room. | | | |

*(continued)*

| Disasters and Catastrophes | Assigned to | Date/Time Assigned | Date/Time Completed |
|---|---|---|---|
| X. Determine and assign sole spokesperson(s) who will be on duty day or night.<br>  1. At site of disaster.<br>  2. At HQ.<br>  3. Different liaison points.<br>  4. "Floater" to make rounds and report continuously via walkie-talkie pertinent calls to HQ PR office. | _____ | _____ | _____ |
| XI. Arrange for switchboard to route all pertinent calls to HQ PR office.<br>  1. Use CB or other communications network. | _____ | _____ | _____ |
| XII. Direct company employees to refrain from making any statement to media people. Only official spokesperson to talk to news media.<br>  1. Request union leaders to cooperate on this. | _____ | _____ | _____ |
| XIII. Inform following that only official spokesperson will issue reliable information:<br>  1. Customers.<br>  2. Dealers.<br>  3. Vendors.<br>  4. Shareholders. | _____ | _____ | _____ |
| XIV. Arrange for news conference as soon as CEO can digest statement.<br>  1. Arrange for CEO interviews with individual press as requested. (See News Conference Checklist.) | _____ | _____ | _____ |
| XV. Arrange for company photographer to obtain complete coverage for legal, file, and news camera people on demand.<br>  2. Arrange for other pertinent interviews, photographs, and TV/radio coverage. | _____ | _____ | _____ |

(continued)

| Disasters and Catastrophes | Assigned to | Date/Time Assigned | Date/Time Completed |
|---|---|---|---|
| 3. Arrange for bios and photos of pertinent employees to be available in press rooms. | | | |
| 4. Obtain, clear, and issue updated, factual news on a continuing basis to all press present and by telephone to others. | | | |
| XVI. Keep news media away from victims, survivors, and relatives until given approval by appropriate persons. | _____ | _____ | _____ |
| 1. Arrange for separate transportation and quarters, if necessary, for victims, survivors, and relatives. | | | |
| 2. Ask hospitals to assign one individual with whom you will coordinate release of information and who will notify you of significant information about injured. | | | |
| XVII. Remember that the sooner you get all the news out, the sooner the catastrophe ceases to be a major news event. | _____ | _____ | _____ |
| 1. Get all the facts. | | | |
| 2. Get all the facts out. | | | |

# 2

# DISSIDENT GROUP ACTIVITY

One way dissident groups in our society try to change the policies and practices of "establishment" institutions is to create crisis situations. In most cases, dissidents are outsiders who select a particular organization as a target in order to achieve a broad social purpose. The target organization may be seen as a particularly bad performer in an area of interest to a dissident group. Other times, the target is chosen because it's big, well known, and an industry leader.

The tactics of dissident groups range from mild forms of informational picketing to outright violence. In all cases, a part of their strategy is to attract media attention and create a crisis of public opinion. Organizations dependent on marketing their products, getting government contracts, keeping the price of their securities high, and recruiting qualified personnel are particularly vulnerable.

**THIRD SECTOR** As this "third sector" has grown to formidable proportions, public relations practitioners have been called upon to deal with them. They are the "new publics" requiring special analysis and treatment.

To begin with, dissident groups vary widely in their purpose and style. Management can be advised to meet with and negotiate with some groups and to avoid and outmaneuver others. It's wise to differentiate among three types of groups:

1. Reformists—They want to gradually improve the system by engaging in moderate levels of protest such as lawful demonstrations and boycotts. Over a third of Americans are said to fall into this category.

2. Activists—They are impatient to get things changed . . . now. They'll use the ballot box and ask government to intervene or they'll use all but the most violent forms of protest.

3. Protesters—These are extremists who have given up on the system and often have a commitment to action for its own sake. While they have no special ideological attachment, they are mobilized to work for specific causes.

Reformists and activists can usually be dealt with on a basis of reason; protesters typically cannot. Engaging in a dialogue with the first two types of groups can help resolve an issue. On the other hand, a strategy may be followed of isolating a protest group by exposing them as societal deviants.

**ASSESSING POWER**  How much latitude management has to deal with dissident groups depends largely on their political resources and the tactics they use. A public relations practitioner should keep a file on each group likely to be confronted. Neighboring companies, the Chamber of Commerce, and trade associations may be able to provide information.

A particularly helpful source is the Foundation for Public Affairs' *Public Interest Profiles* (1220 Sixteen St., NW, Washington, DC 20036). It analyzes 100 organizations. Its contents are of value because they identify important power resources:

► Key staff members.
► Staff size.
► Current budget.
► Scope of activity.
► Basic purpose.

► Method of operations.
► Political orientation.
► Publications.
► Board membership.
► Funding sources.
► Future agenda.
► Analysis of effectiveness of organization.

This checklist highlights three aspects of handling dissident groups: (1) maintaining security and freedom of passage, (2) showing a willingness to negotiate with reasonable dissident leaders, and (3) dealing with the media.

| Dissident Group Activities | Assigned to | Date/Time Assigned | Date/Time Completed |
|---|---|---|---|
| I. Notify the following when any dissident group activity of any sort occurs:<br>1. Local police to request immediate unimpeded passage of employees, visitors, and freight.<br>2. Meet with the following to determine reasons, causes, and possible solutions:<br>  a. CEO.<br>  b. Legal counsel.<br>  c. Union leaders.<br>  d. Head of security.<br>  e. Facility manager.<br>  f. Community leaders.<br>3. Brief all personnel who might become involved. | _____ | _____ | _____ |
| II. Prepare and issue statement of company policy and plans to media.<br>1. Give statement to appropriate police (local/state) for information.<br>2. Instruct company personnel to say nothing to media other than official statement.<br>3. All press inquiries to be funneled to PR office. | _____ | _____ | _____ |
| III. Invite leaders of dissident group to come in to discuss situation with CEO, legal counsel, and Director of Public Relations (DPR). | _____ | _____ | _____ |
| IV. Prepare and issue statement of results of meeting (management's statement of why it's doing what it is doing) to media. | _____ | _____ | _____ |
| V. Notify employees by bulletin board and public address system of company's stand or policy and the reasons for it—in simple, declarative language. Also list demands and reasons of dissenters. | _____ | _____ | _____ |

(continued)

| **Dissident Group Activities** | **Assigned to** | **Date/Time Assigned** | **Date/Time Completed** |
|---|---|---|---|
| VI. Limit company photograph-taking to those for legal use only. | _____ | _____ | _____ |
| VII. Treat mass picketing and vandalism as a police matter, after notification has been made via No Trespassing signs and similar announcements via bulletins. | _____ | _____ | _____ |
|     1. Advise all company personnel to "keep hands off" and leave matters to the police. | | | |
|     2. Emphatically remind all individuals that under no circumstances must any employee, contractor personnel, or any agent connected with the organization physically touch any protester. | | | |
| VIII. Assign one spokesperson to deal with news media, electronic, print, or photography. | _____ | _____ | _____ |
| IX. Update information or statements on a continuous basis so that word of progress comes only from DPR or designee. | _____ | _____ | _____ |
|     1. Arrange press interview for CEO and news media so desiring. | | | |

# 3

# LITIGATION

Ours is a litigious society. Use of legal suits by the average citizen and public interest groups is on the rise. Their aim is to stop objectionable projects and practices and to seek remedies for grievances and injury.

**PUBLIC INTEREST LAW**
Public interest law took hold in the 1960s and 1970s. Public interest groups see recourse to the courts as a quicker process than waiting until an appropriate official takes action or new laws make their way through the legislative mill. Here are some examples:

► The Litigation Group, Ralph Nader's courtroom arm of Public Citizen, protects consumer and worker rights. For example, it represented a union steward who was disciplined for complaining to federal agencies about safety defects.

► Chicago-based Business and Professional People for the Public Interest provides legal representation to groups that might otherwise be unrepresented on issues such as "destruction of the environment by industrial polluters."

17

▶ Center for Law and Social Policy, based in Washington, DC, represents the occupational safety and health interests of mine workers through "participation in legislative reform efforts, federal rule-making, and administration and federal court litigation."

**PR ROLE** Litigation is another kind of crisis. It involves public relations in two ways:

**1.** The mass media are attracted to "big cases" and "human interest" cases. Public relations practitioners must work with the media to obtain fair treatment.

**2.** Litigation can sometimes be avoided when the sued organization is responsive to the feelings, attitudes, values, and goals of its publics. Public relations provides the feedback mechanism from society to a particular organization. When it fails to identify and resolve an issue, aggrieved persons and groups may use the legal route.

**PR AND LAWYERS** A highly publicized antitrust or a product liability case can overnight undo years of effort to humanize a company and establish it as socially responsible. A familiar media stereotype is that of a big, powerful, profit-greedy company devouring its smaller competitors. In the Pinto case, for example, Ford was portrayed as willing to sacrifice lives in order to save a few cents in manufacturing costs.

Lawyers and public relations practitioners must be partners in litigation situations. Lawyers have the tendency to hold back and say nothing to the media out of fear of incriminating the client. They fail to consider the impact on public opinion—and perhaps on the jury. Public relations practitioners want to defend the organization in the court of public opinion by explaining its actions.

In legally sensitive situations, news releases and other public statements must be cleared with legal counsel. But the latter must recognize public relations trade-offs: "no comment" is interpreted by the public that the company has something to hide.

**DISCOURAGING LITIGATION**  Can litigation be discouraged by using public relations as a preventative? Misunderstandings can cause litigation. As communicators, practitioners should be able to remove misunderstandings. Another thing they can do is to identify emerging issues that may cause conflicts. By monitoring the thinking and actions of social action groups, consumers, employees, stockholders, minority and women's groups, practitioners can recommend revisions of organizational policies.

Checklists dealing with dissident group activities, consumer affairs, employee and labor relations, and financial relations are pertinent. They indicate the need for feedback systems and attempts to negotiate with aggrieved groups.

One thing is clear: the new norm in society is to hold its institutions liable for loss of life, property, or rights. People and groups are learning to cope with society's mounting problems by blaming powerful institutions and extracting punishment.

| Litigation | Assigned to | Date/Time Assigned | Date/Time Completed |
|---|---|---|---|
| I.  Prepare for litigation since, in today's litigious climate, none is immune to legal action, merited or not. | _____ | _____ | _____ |
| II.  Identify the organization's areas of vulnerability to law suits. Categorize and check these areas:<br>1.  Products.<br>  a.  Implied or inherent warranties.<br>  b.  Safety caveats in labeling or advertising.<br>  c.  Support of distributors and retail outlets.<br>  d.  Possible recalls of those products which could cause trouble.<br>2.  Product distribution.<br>  a.  Check out sales to controversial countries or areas.<br>  b.  Investigate product safety for international sales if restricted in the United States.<br>  c.  Check on over-zealous marketers who could "dump" products not allowed to be sold here.<br>3.  Investigate and assess complaints received by organization or distribution network.<br>  a.  Establish a system of having all product complaints sent to PR department.<br>  b.  Discuss relevant ones with legal department for vulnerability and probability of litigation.<br>4.  Keep all personnel or organization alert and aware of legal possibilities in product processes and claims.<br>5.  Discuss with CEO and legal department cost ratios in recalls of products, before incidents vis-a-vis after incidents, and resultant court judgments, and then modify product. | _____ | _____ | _____ |

*(continued)*

| Litigation | Assigned to | Date/Time Assigned | Date/Time Completed |
|---|---|---|---|
| III. Organizational policies and attitudes: | _____ | _____ | _____ |
|   1. Recognize contrasting approaches between legal and public relations departments. | | | |
|     a. Legal: Silence. | | | |
|     b. PR: Outspokenness. | | | |
|   2. Monitor the attitudes and actions of dissident groups, consumer groups, employee and labor groups, political expedients, etc. | | | |
|   3. Issue no statements without clearance from legal department. | | | |
|     a. Argue the value of public relations vs. waiting a reactive court battle. | | | |
|   4. Improve your feedback capability so that the company is aware of current feelings toward it. | | | |
| IV. Never forget that in today's ambience, the norm is to hold others liable for loss of life, property, rights, or supposed encroachments. | _____ | _____ | _____ |
| V. Discourage litigation by stating clearly and unambiguously, all corporate philosophies and policies. Also insist publicly that all company products and their warranties are designed in the public interest. | _____ | _____ | _____ |

# II

# CONTINGENCY PLANS

Natural disasters and other randomly occurring catastrophes cannot be avoided. For these, contingency plans must be prepared. A set of programs is designed during a period of noncrisis for every uncertain event that might occur. These written plans define the role of every individual who is involved in a given situation. Basic requirements of such plans are:

- ► Clearly identify the circumstances that deserve the label of disaster, catastrophe, or emergency. Some will be self-evident. Others, as the ambiguities at Three Mile Island, require specific definition.
- ► Assign the crisis designation decision to a specific person or group of persons.
- ► Establish a central crisis information center.
- ► Identify a single spokesperson, who should normally be the public relations director or public information manager.
- ► Decide on the parameters of information that can be released.

"Speaking with a single voice" is critical in crisis situations because these two ingredients of rumors are present: (1) high level of anxiety among people, and (2) high level of ambiguity about what is really happening. The second factor is controllable to the extent that people place confidence in the information disseminated by a central source. If such information is reassuring by at least indicating that the situation is under control, anxiety will be reduced.

The handling of the Three Mile Island incident cautions us not to be reassuring when facts don't justify such an assessment. Understandably, company officers and public officials need to avoid panic and want to avert an evacuation of an area. But an accurate, prudent decision on the seriousness of a situation must be made by the proper authorities. Then the appropriate contingency plan can be followed upon announcement by the designated spokesperson.

# 4

# PREPARING FOR EMERGENCIES

A practitioner must exercise imagination and engage in solid research to prepare plans for emergencies. Imagination identifies what is possible, even when probabilities of occurrence are remote. The idea of all managers who encounter contingencies must be solicited.

Research into the organization's and industry's past yields further traces of what can happen in the future. Newspaper files are a particularly good source. Talks with insurance industry representatives can also be instructive.

Once contingencies are identified, plans are drafted of who does what and when. A key feature of these plans is that a "collateral organization" is established. Specified persons are told that in the event of an emergency they are part of a temporary group with definite tasks to perform.

| Preparing for Emergencies | Assigned to | Date/Time Assigned | Date/Time Completed |
|---|---|---|---|
| I.  Develop a "worst case" list by checking the following for their ideas of the most awful thing that can be imagined happening to the organization:<br>  1. CEO.<br>  2. Department heads.<br>    a. Personnel.<br>    b. Security.<br>    c. Financial.<br>    d. Marketing.<br>    e. Legal.<br>    f. Production.<br>  3. Union leaders.<br>  4. Community leaders.<br>  5. Police and fire departments in each plant community. | \_\_\_\_\_ | \_\_\_\_\_ | \_\_\_\_\_ |
| II.  Review news files and clippings of past emergency situations in your industry.<br>  1. Consult other organizations in your community.<br>  2. Check news desks of national and local media. | \_\_\_\_\_ | \_\_\_\_\_ | \_\_\_\_\_ |
| III.  Compile and consolidate lists for a master list.<br>  1. Categorize them into a few groups for comprehensive contingency plans. | \_\_\_\_\_ | \_\_\_\_\_ | \_\_\_\_\_ |
| IV.  Begin with the constants which will pertain in all cases. These must include:<br>  1. Assignments for PR staff.<br>  2. Listing of all organization personnel who must be notified.<br>  3. Prioritize this list.<br>  4. Create action plan for PR and alternate plans.<br>    a. Establish HQ staff and tasks.<br>    b. Establish field staff and tasks.<br>    c. Establish liaision staff for police, hospitals, etc. | \_\_\_\_\_ | \_\_\_\_\_ | \_\_\_\_\_ |

*(continued)*

| | Preparing for Emergencies | Assigned to | Date/Time Assigned | Date/Time Completed |
|---|---|---|---|---|
| 5. | Arrange and get approval for CEO's actions and statements in emergency. | | | |
| 6. | Assign organization spokesperson and alternates or 24-hour, seven-day duty "T.D." (Until Done). | | | |
| 7. | Print up basic plan(s) and distribute to all departments and divisions with CEO's message that the list must be conspicuously displayed and followed to the letter. Each recipient of the plan must know that he or she must call the notification list in order, beginning with police first, then PR which will pick-up the rest of the calls. | | | |
| 8. | Station lists must be simple, direct, easy-stepped, and quickly implementable. | | | |
| 9. | The PR staff list will be the most comprehensive. | | | |
| 10. | Prepare alternate plans. | | | |
| | a. The plan for an explosion will not fit the plan for combatting a wildcat strike. | | | |
| | b. Each plan must comprise the basic group with the added specifications for its category. | | | |
| 11. | Remember peripheral impact areas, e.g., the advertising department which must have a substitute ad campaign ready for use on being triggered by an emergency. No full-page ads about the safety record of the "Blank Airline" when the front page has the details of a fatal crash. No TV ditties about the "healthful" ingredients of "Bloated Crunchies" when the news segment is blasting a warning by the FDA about Crunchies. | | | |

*(continued)*

| | Preparing for Emergencies | Assigned to | Date/Time Assigned | Date/Time Completed |
|---|---|---|---|---|
| V. | Prepare and get approval for "time-gainer" responses for executives. These are to be used only until a real and factual response is rapidly readied and released. | _____ | _____ | _____ |
| VI. | See checklists on:<br>   a.  News releases.<br>   b.  Disasters and catastrophes.<br>   c.  Strikes and labor activities.<br>   d.  Product boycott.<br>   e.  Dissident group activities. | _____ | _____ | _____ |

# 5

# SEARCH FOR AREAS OF VULNERABILITY

A major activity of public relations is surveillance of the environment. That's what all communication specialists do. Journalists do it to report on the news. The chief reason public relations people do it is to search for areas of vulnerabilities.

Public relations practitioners are interested in certain kinds of information about their organization's environment:

► What publics are in a position to help or hurt the organization? The list should include conventional publics, e.g., stockholders, employers, community citizens, government officials, as well as activist groups in the so-called third sector that seek to change corporate behavior.

► What opinions do these publics—and the general public—hold toward the organization?
Are attitudes generally favorable or unfavorable?
What are their expectations of the organization?
Do they feel the organizations measure up to these expectations?

If not, how strongly do they feel about the gap between expectations and performances?

What actions, if any, are they likely to take?

► What are the media saying about your organization and industry?

Are accusations of government officials or dissident groups reported?

Is the reporting biased?

Are investigative reporters probing into your organization or industry?

► Are laws or regulations affecting your industry being considered by federal, state, or local legislators or officials?

Will such actions be harmful?

At what stage in the public policy process are these laws and regulations?

In addition to monitoring the external socio-political environment, practitioners should examine data from a variety of internal feedback systems. These data may be collected by the public relations department or by a lateral staff organization such as the personnel/industrial relations, consumer affairs, or investor relations department. For example, employee relations indices include:

► High number of grievances.
► High turnover rate.
► High absenteeism.
► Low readership of employee publications.
► Union organizing activity.

| Search for Areas of Vulnerability | Assigned to | Date/Time Assigned | Date/Time Completed |
|---|---|---|---|
| I. Go over each checklist for sensitive spots where anticipation can help prepare your organization to combat trouble. | _____ | _____ | _____ |
| II. Do your homework on current events. Check your organization for the troubles besetting other companies in the news. | _____ | _____ | _____ |
| III. Aggressively, and in adversary mode, look for areas on which your company can be attacked, including:<br>1. Actions.<br>2. Attitudes.<br>3. Policies.<br>4. Production methods.<br>5. Products.<br>6. Non-actions. | _____ | _____ | _____ |
| IV. Keep updated on, and check your vulnerability on:<br>1. New laws—federal and local.<br>2. Federal and local regulations and statutes.<br>3. Pollution.<br>   a. Air.<br>   b. Ground.<br>   c. Water.<br>4. OSHA.<br>5. Affirmative action.<br>6. Employee expectations or unrest.<br>7. Market trends.<br>8. Financial trends.<br>9. Take-over susceptibility. | _____ | _____ | _____ |
| V. Check your industry, professional, or other association for indications of trouble to organizations similar to yours. | _____ | _____ | _____ |
| VI. Scrutinize every plant, facility, department, and division during regular visits. (See "Parish" Calls, Chapter 52.) | _____ | _____ | _____ |

*(continued)*

| Search for Areas of Vulnerability | Assigned to | Date/Time Assigned | Date/Time Completed |
|---|---|---|---|
| VII. Check your organization's involvement and investments in geographical or political areas of concern to those fighting Third World or other causes. | _____ | _____ | _____ |
| VIII. Report violations, transgressions, or borderline cases which could result in unfavorable reaction by any pertinent public, to plant or division manager, legal officer, and eventually to CEO, with suggested solutions. Examples include: <br> 1. Lights or noises from company buildings, which disturb neighborhood. <br> 2. Employee auto traffic adversely affecting community traffic patterns. <br> 3. Survey of blacks, Hispanics, Orientals, handicapped, women at various levels of company structure. <br> 4. Efforts taken to assure equitable representation. <br> 5. Survey of number and types of accidents in facilities. <br> 6. Assessment of employees' most common complaints. <br> 7. Review of products and services in light of consumer group activities. | _____ | _____ | _____ |
| IX. Assess organization's ethics. <br> 1. Is there a clearly and emphatically stated ethical policy? <br> 2. Is it written and spelled out for each new hire? <br> 3. Who observes its compliance? <br> 4. Is it observed or merely given lip-service? <br> 5. Does the CEO demand strict enforcement of policy? | _____ | _____ | _____ |

*(continued)*

| Search for Areas of Vulnerability | Assigned to | Date/Time Assigned | Date/Time Completed |
|---|---|---|---|
| 6. Are violators' discharges or censures made known throughout the company? | | | |
| 7. How often does the organization hold ethics seminars? | | | |
| X. Advertising truth. | —— | —— | —— |
|   1. Is your advertising department and its agency aware of all company policies, taboos, limitations, and restrictions? | | | |
|   2. Do company advertisements, corporate and product, reflect a true image of the organization? | | | |
| XI. Shareholder knowledge: | —— | —— | —— |
|   1. Goals. | | | |
|   2. Policies. | | | |
|   3. Personnel. | | | |
|   4. Products. | | | |
|   5. Facilities. | | | |
|   6. Geographical spread. | | | |
|   7. Communities impacted. | | | |
|   8. Industry standing. | | | |
|   9. Financial status. | | | |

# III

# MEDIA RELATIONS

The news release and press conference symbolize public relations for many people. Actually, they are the chief tools of an important part of public relations known as publicity or media relations.

Historically, companies hired journalists to write favorable stories about them to offset a "bad press." These journalists were known as press agents. They served as advocates for an organization. Publicity became the vehicle for bringing favorable attention to a person, idea, product, or organization in the mass media and other specialized media.

A knowledge of what media exist, what audiences they reach, and what editors and producers are interested in publishing or broadcasting is fundamental to publicity work. Publicists must have a sense of what is newsworthy. They are more likely to develop this "instinct" by first working for a newspaper and then transferring to public relations. For a while at least, their contacts may facilitate the acceptance of their news releases. But a professional publicist knows that ultimately the interests of media audiences must be satisfied.

As publicity evolved into counseling of management, a profound change occurred. Managers learned that the only way to build public understanding of their organizations was to be more open—do good and talk about it. Willingness to disclose information remains a basic thrust of public relations. This willingness has to be balanced against the requirements of confidentiality and rights of privacy.

Most media complaints about publicity releases center around the providing of inadequate and self-serving information. The public media cannot be treated as if they were extensions of an organization's employee communications network. A recent survey conducted by one of the authors shows that the messages public relations directors are most interested in bringing to the attention of the media are:

1. Corporate social responsibility programs.

2. Environmental achievement and the need for trade-offs.

3. Human side of corporate life, personal glimpses of management.

4. Research, technical achievements, innovations.

5. Positions on legislative or regulatory matters.

6. Employee recognition.

The news media not only want more information but crave controversy. They see themselves in an adversary role with newsmakers and sources. Hence a degree of tension characterizes media relations, which is summed up in the last checklist on ambient press hostility.

# NEWS RELEASES

Someone once commented that publicity was the tool chest of the public relations practitioner. If that is so, then the news release is certainly the hammer in that chest.

It is the means of communication and without it there is no dissemination of the desired information about the organization. And since this is an accepted fact of life, the news desks of all types of news media are daily swamped with hundreds of news releases and so-called news stories.

It is virtually impossible for any news editor to read through all of these missives—many of which are marked "urgent." The editor immediately becomes a "triageur," consigning 90 percent of the "news releases" to the waste basket. And the problem then facing the public relations practitioner is how to keep his or her releases from being discarded, either unread or misunderstood.

Obviously any news release reaching the desk of an editor must not be irritating at first sight, but just as obviously, as any editor will attest, scores of releases come to him or her with the printed legend "IMPOR-TANT NEWS." The hackle-raised reaction is perfectly natural. In the same category are the releases that help the editor by informing him or her that the release is "Front Page News."

Other irritants include: the release with already written headlines; over-written material (some are five pages long, when one suffices); the release which always begins with the name of the CEO of the issuing organization; the advertisement for a product which is barely disguised as news; and those with ham-handed pretentiousness or glowing purple phrases.

All minor and none of any significance, but it must be remembered that there seems to be a natural adversary relationship between public relations people and news people. Perhaps justified and perhaps not. In any case, it becomes an insult to editors not to pay close attention to what annoys them.

At the very least, a news release writer should make some effort to make his or her output professional looking, so that it will be read—and will not irritate the recipient. It would seem to be only common sense to make a news release—or any product for that matter—as much like what people want as possible. The old Henry Ford cliche syndrome of "You can have any color car you want as long as it's black," should be avoided.

One of the most common faults in news release writing is mailing out non-news. Example: "Eben J. Wasserhalter has just been promoted to third vice president in charge of the Black Company's plant in Puccini, Idaho, which employs eleven people."

Justifying one's public relations department's budget by scaling it to the poundage of news releases issued is a certain avenue to personal release—from the organization.

One of the greatest attributes of a publicity person is the ability to divorce one's self from the subjectivity of the company and to assess news values correctly.

A personal friendship with a wire service editor is no guarantee that a border-line news story will be used. No editor, if he or she wants to keep working, will use non-stories, even for a twin brother or sister. Conversely, the editor will use a real story even if it comes from someone for whom he or she has no personal regard.

| News Releases | Assigned to | Date/Time Assigned | Date/Time Completed |
|---|---|---|---|
| I.  Advise management and all pertinent executives that no news releases will be sent out unless they are actual news and not personal puffs. | _____ | _____ | _____ |
| II.  Instruct your staff to observe these fundamentals of format: | _____ | _____ | _____ |

II.  Instruct your staff to observe these fundamentals of format:

   1.  No headlines.

   2.  Story starts 1/3 way down the page.

   3.  Double spacing and proper margins (1 inch).

   4.  Break no paragraphs between lines or pages.

   5.  Break no proper names between lines or pages.

   6.  Second page (others) is numbered in upper left corner followed by one word slug indicating content.

   7.  On top of page one indicate whom release is from, with address, day and night phone numbers for further information.

   8.  On the other corner show release date and time.

   9.  Forget stylish writing. Use straightforward AP style of statement of facts, with principal ingredients of news in the first line. Lead paragraph, except in unusual circumstances, should not exceed sixteen lines. Get style books from AP and *New York Times.*

  10.  Use a dictionary. Also suggested is Curtis D. MacDougall's *Interpretative Reporting.*

  11.  End each page of story that is continued with "(more,)" and end the story with "###."

*(continued)*

| News Releases | Assigned to | Date/Time Assigned | Date/Time Completed |
|---|---|---|---|
| 12. If photo or illustration accompanies story, mark "with art" in left bottom corner under "###." | | | |
| 13. Except for unusual situations, keep story length to not more than two pages. | | | |
| III. Prepare your news release in such a way that it is acceptable and will be read. Remember that every news desk receives hundreds of releases every day. | _____ | _____ | _____ |
| IV. Instruct your writers to eliminate writing that is obviously disguised advertising or promotion. Use fact and leave out editorials. | _____ | _____ | _____ |
| V. Keep your writers ever-mindful of the news dictum that the lead paragraphs must contain, in order of importance,<br>1. What?<br>2. Who?<br>3. Where?<br>4. When?<br>5. Why?<br>6. How? | _____ | _____ | _____ |
| VI. It is not necessary to begin every story with the name of the chief executive officer. | _____ | _____ | _____ |
| VII. For TV and radio news desks, the information in item V is all they'll need unless they want to do a feature, in which case they'll ask. | _____ | _____ | _____ |
| VIII. Maintain your sincerity and integrity by supplying facts on negative or adverse stories about your company without waiting to be called about them. Don't try to hide such information. It will be discovered and you'll wind up with a bad story. | _____ | _____ | _____ |

(continued)

| **News Releases** | **Assigned to** | **Date/Time Assigned** | **Date/Time Completed** |
|---|---|---|---|
| IX. It is perfectly proper to write your story with the attitude that "The glass is half full" rather than "The glass is half empty." | _____ | _____ | _____ |
| X. Make certain that the news release will be delivered before the release date and time.<br>   1. Use multiple phone calls in case time sequence prevents proper delivery.<br>   2. Query significant news media for special and specific needs. | _____ | _____ | _____ |

# 7

# PRESS KITS

Possibilities for comments out of context, inaccurate quotations, misspelled names, wrong attributions, misunderstood speeches, and other errors can be minimized by the proper preparation of so-called press kits. They should be used each time there is a news conference, or at any other event which brings out media coverage.

Some organizations go overboard with elaborate, embossed cover product which is usually too expensive and sometimes embarrassing. Other companies swing to the other extreme and hand out loose batches of papers and photographs. A cover-stock folder with a turned up bottom will hold all the material necessary for the press kit. It will also give a business-like appearance and will satisfy the print and electronic news persons covering the affair or event.

There is a temptation to keep adding material to the kit even though it may be barely relevant. Resist it and include only that material that is directly concerned with the affair. If any media person wants more information, extended detail or facts for a feature, he or she will ask for it.

It generally is not necessary to insert the CEO's photograph in every press kit. It is necessary, however, to put into the kit all illustrative material and artwork that will make plain the purposes of the conference or event.

Occasionally, in the case of the introduction of a new product, process, or service, sample units or ingredients or even mechanical breakaway sketches should be included.

For affairs relative to the financial community, the inclusion of "bar" or "pie" charts is recommended. So, too, are architect's elevations for news conferences called for the announcement of new facilities or plants.

| Press Kits | Assigned to | Date/Time Assigned | Date/Time Completed |
|---|---|---|---|
| I. Recognize the need for take-away and reference material at each press conference and other media-covered event by preparing a pocketed folder which will include: | _____ | _____ | _____ |
|   1. An adhesive label for the outside bearing the company name, subject, name of Director of Public Relations (DPR) or other PR staff person, with phone numbers (day/night). | | | |
|   2. Copy of principal speeches. | | | |
|   3. Back up technical reference material buttressing speech facts. | | | |
|   4. Photo of speaker(s) with attached caption(s) and short separate biography(ies). | | | |
|   5. If there is a separate "expert" or "inventor," include his or her photo, caption, and biography. | | | |
|   6. Short company history for background frame, including number of employees, annual payroll, etc., as well as list of products, industry and financial status, annual sales, and order backlog, etc. | | | |
|   7. If the subject of the conference will increase employee count, payroll, and taxes, indicate these in both dollars and percentages. | | | |
|   8. Include separate statements from VIPs pertinent to the announcement (governor, senators, mayors, etc.) for quotes in the story. | | | |
|   9. Make certain that all those covering events receive kits. | | | |
| II. Make enough copies of the press kit for those not present but who request or should get copies. | _____ | _____ | _____ |
|   1. Send copies to industry and trade publications. | | | |
|   2. Send copies to financial list. | | | |

(continued)

| Press Kits | Assigned to | Date/Time Assigned | Date/Time Completed |
|---|---|---|---|
| 3. Give copies to company publications. | | | |
| 4. Give a kit to each person mentioned in the kit. | | | |
| 5. Send kit to hometown media of those mentioned in the kit. | | | |
| 6. Give a kit to each division, department, and facility manager. | | | |
| 7. Send kit to advertising agency. | | | |
| III. Exclude all non-essential "junk," which many executives in company may request because they believe that bulk makes substance. | _____ | _____ | _____ |

# 8

# PRESS ROOMS

Although press rooms are among the fondest memories of most journalists, and press room stories are legendary and legion, the press room is a working place. As such it needs proper establishment and efficient operation and maintenance.

Despite the congenial atmosphere of most press rooms, the room is actually the working press's office—and must be kept, by those in charge, in a manner conducive to the best working conditions. A quiet, clean, and orderly office space, with all necessary tools, results in a good relationship with the news media and a resultant objective product.

There will be constant pressure on those operating the press room by persons whose connections with the working press are so tenuous as to be nearly invisible. These press "groupies" must be firmly and politely refused admission. The room is for working press only—and their guests.

The public relations staff personnel assigned to the press room must be knowledgeable about the organization and its policies. They must be totally accommodating, but at the same time must be fully alert to their own limitations in speaking about the company for quotation. And they must have a list of persons who will be on call to speak with authority for the organization.

In addition to those who will write their stories in the press room, the electronic media people have need to conduct taping interviews and make videos. A separate room, off the press room proper, should be set up for such purposes. And that room must have proper equipment that will be needed by electronic news media personnel.

On occasion, individual and special interest reporters will want to interview the CEO or other senior officers of the company. Here, too, a special room must be set up. Sometimes, if the event is being held at a hotel or club, a private room can be set aside for this use.

If the press room is set up in connection with a trade show or convention with exhibits, there will be a demand for admission tickets larger than has been expected—and often from people who have no right to ask for them. The PR staff person in charge of this facet is advised to be lenient rather than tough in handing out admission tickets. But working press tickets or badges, which allow entrance at any time and as often as desired, must be kept only to those who are actually covering the affair.

In the case of having to establish a press room to accommodate working news media people as the result of a negative event (disaster, fire, strike, air crash, etc.), an enlarged staff must be assigned to the "Field Press Room." Many more tasks face field public relation staff people since other accommodations are required, such as sleeping quarters and transportation. Do not, at such a happening, attempt to do things "on the cheap."

Provide comfortable, liveable quarters. See that decent meals are provided. Make certain that adequate transportation is offered—to and from the site of the event—as well as for story material and photographs back to the journalists' headquarters. Have a full file of photograph backgrounders and biographies and historical material available and easily obtainable for those covering the event. At these happenings there will be more need for separate rooms for interviews with victims, survivors, and senior organization officers.

| **Press Rooms** | **Assigned to** | **Date/Time Assigned** | **Date/Time Completed** |
|---|---|---|---|
| I. Establish a separate press room for any event, activity, or emergency. <br>   1. Determine size of room needed by estimating the number of press persons who will use it. Include a safety factor of 25 percent for those who come without notification. | _____ | _____ | _____ |
| II. Locate the press room as close to the principal scene of the activity as possible. <br>   1. Make certain it can be locked and secure. | _____ | _____ | _____ |
| III. Arrange for rental typewriters on trestle tables as desks, with adequate supplies of copy paper, carbons, pencils, copying machine, dictionary, pertinent reference books, telephones, a clothes rack, and a bulletin board. | _____ | _____ | _____ |
| IV. Assign two persons to the press room who are cognizant of company policy, and the limitations of their authority, as well as the object and purpose of the event. | _____ | _____ | _____ |
| V. Prepare a press kit for each person who attends. Obviously, the number will exceed the number of typewriters. | _____ | _____ | _____ |
| VI. Arrange for all copies of speeches to be handed out not earlier than one hour before delivery. Have necessary photos and bios ready. | _____ | _____ | _____ |
| VII. Set aside a separate room (small and off the main press room) for private interviews, tapings, audio/visual use, and conversations. | _____ | _____ | _____ |
| VIII. Arrange for an anteroom to the press room in which coffee, sandwiches, soft and hard drinks will be available. Hire a steward. Don't let it become a company personnel club. Close when the press room proper closes. | _____ | _____ | _____ |

*(continued)*

| Press Rooms | Assigned to | Date/Time Assigned | Date/Time Completed |
|---|---|---|---|
| IX. Arrange for incidentals such as:<br>  1. A log for attendees to sign in.<br>  2. A supply of admission tickets. (If it's for a show, don't be reluctant to give tickets to any responsible press person for his or her friends.)<br>  3. Working press tickets should carry I.D. of press person. Consider press name badges. | _____ | _____ | _____ |
| X. Arrange for a press table, up front, for lunches and dinners. | _____ | _____ | _____ |
| IX. If the event is a disaster (air crash, explosion of tank, any outside event away from HQ) set up a PR field office, which will be a press room on location.<br>  1. Arrange for sleeping quarters for press who cover event.<br>  2. Arrange for transportation for press and PR staff to and from field office.<br>  3. Arrange for transportation to and from crisis scene.<br>  4. Arrange dark room facilities.<br>  5. Arrange transport of film, photos, and stories back to city.<br>  6. Assign responsible PR field manager, and assign similar person (DPR) for HQ office.<br>  7. Have photos, biographies of those involved. | _____ | _____ | _____ |
| XII. Have press room open for early arrivals and keep it open one hour after the last press person has left. | _____ | _____ | _____ |
| XIII. Hire someone to maintain a clean, orderly room. Same person can keep ice container filled, etc. | _____ | _____ | _____ |

*(continued)*

| | Press Rooms | Assigned to | Date/Time Assigned | Date/Time Completed |
|---|---|---|---|---|
| XIV. | Hire necessary electricians, electronic personnel to accommodate TV/radio needs. | _____ | _____ | _____ |
| XV. | Set up a TV interviewing room with plain uncluttered background, chairs, desk, table, and products or visual aids. | _____ | _____ | _____ |
| XVI. | Have available properly operating tape recorders for interviews and conferences. | _____ | _____ | _____ |
| XVII. | Have proper screen and projection equipment. | _____ | _____ | _____ |
| XVIII. | Rent a small color TV for press room use. | _____ | _____ | _____ |

# 9

# PRESS INQUIRIES

One of the most awkward areas in the relationship with the news media is that surrounding inquiries from the press. Too often the calling news person is unhappy with the response given by the Director of Public Relations (DPR) and demands to talk to the CEO. When, for no fault of his or her own, the CEO is unable to accept the call, the media person becomes hostile and the result is something along the line of, "The president of the Blank Company refused to answer a direct question."

Of course, if questioners perfectly accepted and trusted the DPR, then they would accept the PR practitioner's response to an inquiry. And it must be recognized by DPRs that journalists who call are under pressure from their news desks to get a "good quote from the head of the company."

The DPR (and through him or her, the CEO) is frequently at a loss as to how to respond to a direct question about, for instance, an acquisition of another company. If both are listed on the big boards, there is the matter of a sharp impact on the shares of both companies, no matter which answer is given to the question, "Are you buying the Whitehitch

Corporation?" If the CEO or DPR says "No," in order not to jeopardize the transaction, and negotiations are really underway, he or she is branded publicly as a liar. If the reply is "Yes," the CEO will probably lose the deal and have the SEC on his or her neck as well. If the answer is "No comment," as many executives have done, he or she is actually indicating an affirmative.

Some companies have devised responses such as "I will neither affirm nor deny and for the reasons which you know." It is then the responsibility of the DPR to see that the questioner is the first person called when there is information available and PR staff then makes calls to all pertinent financial media.

Several years ago a financial editor called an electronics company in the Boston area. He insisted on speaking to the CEO and asked him, "Is it true that you are in secret negotiations to merge with the Ford Motor Company?" When the CEO told him the question was absurd, the editor thanked the CEO. And the next day there was a small item on the financial page of the home city of the company, with the headline "Blank Company denies Ford merger." Not all situations can be circumvented.

Over the long haul the best response to such financial questions —or others which might have a serious impact on the community or labor force—must be "I cannot answer that question." And stick to it.

It is obvious that all inquiries must funnel through the DPR. All company executives must be made aware by the CEO that such is the case. In the case of special knowledge such as legal matters or accounting matters, those department heads will be asked to respond, bearing in mind the organization's posture and policy. When it is necessary for the CEO to be quoted, he or she must be armed with facts and respond in a quotable manner.

When a request comes in to the public relations department for an answer directly from the CEO, the DPR will ask the subject matter and have the CEO apprised of the nature of the query, along with any modifying factors that could affect the answer, and then the CEO must call back as soon as possible.

All calls must be returned within a realistic time and, as far as possible or feasible, answered as fully as the questioner wants.

| **Press Inquiries** | **Assign to** | **Date/Time Assigned** | **Date/Time Completed** |
|---|---|---|---|
| I. Have CEO instruct all managers that all inquiries from news media, print or electronic, must be routed to the DPR—and politely. | _____ | _____ | _____ |
| II. When a call finally reaches the DPR for information of any sort about your organization, make arrangements to have any executive cognizant in the field of query call back the inquirer with a full response—and pleasantly. | _____ | _____ | _____ |
| III. Impress on your executives that it is possible to answer, "I don't know, but I'll try to find out and call you back." Have them be meticulous in calling back. | _____ | _____ | _____ |
| IV. When press calls come directly to the office of the CEO, his or her answer must be a "call back." In the meantime the DPR can be made aware of the inquiry and its subject, and discover any need for modification. | _____ | _____ | _____ |
| V. Be certain that the company policy of returning all press calls within fifteen minutes is followed. | _____ | _____ | _____ |
| VI. Prepare your CEO to respond in such a manner that he or she will be quoted, by name, on matters of company policy. Only in the CEO's absence will the DPR get a transfer of a press call directly to him or her. | _____ | _____ | _____ |
| VII. Inform all managers or staff heads that on occasion, inquiries will be referred to them because of their specialized knowledge, and that they will be quoted by name. Emphasize to them that there are no off-the-record responses and that their answers must be compatible with company posture. | _____ | _____ | _____ |

*(continued)*

| Press Inquiries | Assign to | Date/Time Assigned | Date/Time Completed |
|---|---|---|---|
| VIII. Remember that in many cases the DPR must be the surrogate for the press. It is important to take his or her attitude in developing a response. Consequently, be cheerful and helpful. Do not anticipate and do not assume an adversary relationship with the press person seeking information. | _____ | _____ | _____ |
| IX. Inquiries often will deal with sensitive matters which may be in negotiation or which, for other reasons, cannot be answered with either a yes or no. <br> 1. Don't be afraid to respond, "I cannot answer that." <br> 2. If the questioner is insistent, answer "I cannot answer that because I do not know," or "I cannot answer that at this time." <br> 3. Avoid the cliche response of "No comment." It infuriates news people and, when published or telecast, sounds as if you have something to hide. | _____ | _____ | _____ |
| X. Recognize that on occasion an absurdity is asked in the hope that it will bring about a newsworthy response. Be on guard. | _____ | _____ | _____ |
| XI. Just as often, a baseless rumor begins circulating and can be quashed only by a firm unequivocal response. Get the facts and a very short quotation from the CEO to stop the rumor immediately. | _____ | _____ | _____ |

# 10

# NEWS CONFERENCES

When a news release or press inquiry is inadequate for handling important news, a news conference should be called. This "event" provides an opportunity for newsmakers and reporters to meet on a face-to-face basis. Impressions can be conveyed as well as "hard" information. News people can ask questions to clarify or expand upon announcements made by spokespersons.

News conferences entail risks. If media representatives feel that the news is not important enough to justify their attendance, their resentment will be shown. The news story may be negatively treated and the credibility and judgment of the organization questioned. When the director of public relations tries to call another news conference, fewer media people are likely to show up. Another risk of a news conference is that the situation is only semi-controlled. The presentation of the spokesperson—and perhaps those of others—can and should be decided in advance. Answers to expected questions can be rehearsed, but there is always the possibility of a surprise question or an awkward answer.

Despite these vulnerabilities, the benefits of a well-managed news conference are enormous. Important announcements stand a better chance of winning media attention. Coverage will likely be more accurate and complete.

Many aspects of news conferences are discussed in other chapters, such as the handling of disasters, making new product announcements, and holding conventions and sales meetings. This checklist provides an overview of basic considerations.

| News Conferences | Assigned to | Date/Time Assigned | Date/Time Completed |
|---|---|---|---|
| I.  Determine:<br>   1.  Actual need.<br>   2.  Specific goal.<br>   3.  Product, service, or subject.<br>   4.  Time schedule.<br>   5.  Target audience.<br>      a.  Media list (pertinent).<br>      b.  Other publics: employees, vendors, community, distribution network, financial (stockholders, security analysts), union, suppliers.<br>   6.  Location for conference. | ____ | ____ | ____ |
| II.  Decide on conference site.<br>   1.  Hotel.<br>   2.  Plant or other company facility.<br>   3.  Site of an event in case of disaster or catastrophe. | ____ | ____ | ____ |
| III.  With CEO and pertinent senior officers, determine:<br>   1.  Who will be the company spokesperson(s).<br>   2.  Contents of press kit.<br>   3.  Graphics or visual aids.<br>   4.  List of invitees. | ____ | ____ | ____ |
| IV.  Write draft of principal statement and get clearance from:<br>   1.  CEO.<br>   2.  Legal department.<br>   3.  Marketing department.<br>   4.  Treasurer. | ____ | ____ | ____ |
| V.  Prepare potential Q&A to be expected from attending news media. | ____ | ____ | ____ |
| VI.  For non-emergency press conference:<br>   1.  Begin arrangements at least one month in advance to reserve: | ____ | ____ | ____ |

*(continued)*

| News Conferences | Assigned to | Date/Time Assigned | Date/Time Completed |
|---|---|---|---|
|     a. Conference room.<br>    b. Press room. (See Press Room<br>       Checklist.)<br>  2. Invitations.<br>  3. Advance release, two weeks prior, notifying news conference date and time.<br>  4. Phone calls to those not heard from three days prior to conference. | | | |
| VII. Determine a.m. or p.m. practicality to meet media needs.<br>  1. Check for news deadlines on TV, radio, and print media.<br>  2. If morning, set up refreshments, lunch, etc.<br>  3. If afternoon, set up for possible cocktails after news conference. | _____ | _____ | _____ |
| VIII. If emergency situation, follow Disasters and Catastrophes Checklist. | _____ | _____ | _____ |
| IX. For mechanical details, see Conventions and Sales Meeting Checklist. | _____ | _____ | _____ |
| X. For material for "handout and take-away," see Press Kit Checklist, News Release Checklist, New Product Announcements Checklist, and TV/Radio Appearance Checklist. | _____ | _____ | _____ |

# CLEARANCE FORMS

This is an era of litigation; a period when lawsuits dominate. It is a time of suing for vast amounts of money; a time when jury awards are no longer page one news. It seems that everyone is alert for the smallest of errors, the slightest of infractions, to bring out avarice—and lawyers—with unconscionable demands for "compensation."

In such an ambient climate, public relations practitioners, their organizations, and their clients need to exert extreme care in not leaving themselves vulnerable to legal action by the ommision of getting clearance or permission to use names, photographs, video, tape, quotations, etc.

Standard clearance forms (in some cases called, "PTQ's" for Permission to Quote) are available and effective in keeping clear of claims and courtrooms. It is wise to emphasize to all employees of organizations that the use of such clearance forms is a necessity and also that those who do not get them signed, either from carelessness, forgetfulness, or preoccupation, will be likely to find themselves personally party to suits for "damages."

The forms to be used must be issued to all staff, whether writer, photographer, or liaison person, together with an explanatory note from the legal department.

| Clearance Forms | Assigned to | Date/Time Assigned | Date/Time Completed |
|---|---|---|---|
| I. Obtain from your legal department a standard, short release form for use on photography, advertisements, quotations, and attributions. | _____ | _____ | _____ |
| II. See that your advertising agency uses the same forms that you do. | _____ | _____ | _____ |
| III. Advise all company officers, facility managers, and other pertinent personnel that these forms must be used before any picture or quotation can be publicly released. | _____ | _____ | _____ |
| IV. Instruct your staff that no photograph of anyone or any object be released without full and correct names, addresses, and identification; that no photograph, filmstrip, video material, tape recording, quotation, or attribution can be released without first obtaining proper clearance signatures. | _____ | _____ | _____ |
| V. Provide all organization's photographers, still and motion, with pads of such forms for quick use in the field. Also supply them to stringers and any hired camera crew. | _____ | _____ | _____ |
| VI. Remember that signatures must be obtained from employees when their pictures are used in general releases, in company publications of any sort, or in trade, industry, or professional publication. They must also be used when employees, even unnamed, are used in company advertising. | _____ | _____ | _____ |

# 12

# MEDIA LISTS

The old philosophical cliché postulating that a tree falling in the forest, unheard, has not fallen, is a most apt analog for the well-written and meaningful news message that is undisseminated.

To mail out news releases under conditions other than those totally controlled is of doubtful value. The most successful public relations managers are those who establish and maintain a system of distribution using media lists compiled to include every single outlet that can benefit the organization, and in a format desired by each of the media.

There are about a dozen directories that provide lists of various types of publications, their requirements, deadlines, physical formats, frequency of publication, and readerships. DPR's use these directories as a base for their media lists and add to them the special outlets pertinent to their needs.

Some publications are interested only in specific data and figures; others demand analysis wth the news releases; still others will not use photographs of products. Some refuse to use photographs at all.

In using mats for broad distribution of artwork (charts, graphs, etc.), one must be aware of the width of the columns in the publication.

Many television station news editors avoid using still photographs. Others will not accept filmstrips in any form.

Occasionally an editor will not accept or use material unless it is addressed to him or her by name. In other cases, news desks require all material be sent to the desk only. All these idiosyncracies must be recognized and accommodated.

A proper media list file will encompass all of these needs and will be established in categories so that the mailing department, or outside mailing house, need only be supplied with a code number or numbers that gives all the information necessary to achieve full and proper distribution of news and feature releases. In addition, this code should be printed at the bottom of each release, together with the date, so that one has a record of who got the release, when, and with or without photography or artwork.

The media lists must be "cleaned" periodically to eliminate waste which, under present postal costs, becomes substantial. This also avoids the irritant of having news releases arrive at a news desk addressed to someone no longer with the company.

In every media list file there should also be a list of those persons, both within the company and outside of it, to whom specific releases should be sent. And be certain that you add your clipping service(s) to every distribution list and for every release.

| Media Lists | Assigned to | Date/Time Assigned | Date/Time Completed |
|---|---|---|---|
| I. Arrange your media source files in categories. | _____ | _____ | _____ |
| II. Obtain national media list books: | _____ | _____ | _____ |
|    1. *Bacon's Publicity Checker.* | | | |
|    2. *N. W. Ayer Directory of Newspapers and Periodicals.* | | | |
|    3. *Standard Rate and Data Services directories.* | | | |
|    4. *Editor and Publisher International Year Book.* | | | |
|    5. *Gebbie's House Magazine Directory.* | | | |
|    6. *The Working Press of the Nation.* | | | |
|    7. *Broadcasting Yearbook.* | | | |
| III. Obtain regional and local media list books such as: | _____ | _____ | _____ |
|    1. *NYC Press and TV Contracts.* | | | |
|    2. *Washington Press Club Contact List.* | | | |
| IV. Prepare category lists including: | _____ | _____ | _____ |
|    1. City editors. | | | |
|    2. Special and feature editors, writers, and photographers. | | | |
|    3. Financial editors and columnists. | | | |
|    4. Financial analysts. | | | |
|    5. Special stockholders. | | | |
|    6. Specific trade publication editors. | | | |
|    7. Photographers. | | | |
|    8. Freelance writers. | | | |
|    9. Plant community media editors. | | | |
|   10. TV and radio news assignment editors—national and local. | | | |
|   11. Opinion leaders. | | | |
|   12. Congressional, state, and local leaders. | | | |
|   13. Union leaders. | | | |
|   14. Pertinent newsletter editors. | | | |
|   15. House organ editors. | | | |

*(continued)*

| Media Lists | Assigned to | Date/Time Assigned | Date/Time Completed |
|---|---|---|---|
| 16. Wire service bureau chiefs. | | | |
| 17. Specific special interest writers and photographers. | | | |
| 18. Syndicate heads. | | | |
| 19. Clipping bureaus. | | | |
| 20. Weekly news magazines: editors, writers, and columnists. | | | |
| 21. General business magazines and publications. | | | |
| V. Establish each of these lists in your files with specific numbers or codes. | _____ | _____ | _____ |
| VI. Include in each list—for each medium: | _____ | _____ | _____ |
| 1. Photo requirements. | | | |
| 2. Special editorial requirements. | | | |
| 3. Deadlines. | | | |
| 4. Formats. | | | |
| 5. Submission locally or to main office, or both. | | | |
| VII. Include in each list action dates (deadlines and lead time). | _____ | _____ | _____ |
| VIII. Make enough copies of each category for staff use, and for distribution net (printer/mailer). | _____ | _____ | _____ |
| IX. Be sure to have check-off boxes clear and unmistakable on each list for specific requirements. | _____ | _____ | _____ |
| X. Clean and update your list files on a regular basis. Use post-paid return cards to "clear" the lists every six months or once a year. | _____ | _____ | _____ |
| XI. Put appropriate and pertinent persons in the company and industry on the courtesy mailing list. | _____ | _____ | _____ |
| XII. Have every release carry, on the bottom, a list indicator and date code for the distribution organization as well as for files. | _____ | _____ | _____ |

# 13

# CLIPPING SERVICES

One of life's more unsatisfactory aspects is to say something significant and be rewarded with an absolute lack of response. It is something like shouting at a known "echo" spot and then hearing only silence. So, too, in sending out important news releases and to hear no "echo"—it is the same as not having sent out any releases at all.

Clipping services will inform you whether or not you have been heard. Although the knowledge that what has been released has been received and printed is a major reason for employing a clipping service, there are other values from such a service.

The effectiveness of the release can be determined by the ratio of clippings returned; by the "play" that the release received in various news media; the types of publications, wire services, and electronic media that used the information sent out, and eventually the response of the publics on which the release impinged.

If photographs were included with the news release, the returned clippings will indicate, by the number of news media that used them, how they were cropped. They will also show the emphasis generally placed on individual parts of the photograph—the skill in pictorial judgment of public relations staff personnel.

Occasionally, the DPR will be astonished by a huge return of clippings on a release that seemed routine, and whose message was relatively minor. Conversely, there are times when a scant minimum of clippings result from a mailing.

Although it is highly satisfying to the writer and photographer to get clippings back that can be measured by the pound, enlightened management today realizes that quality rather than quantity counts in release use. And the page-one use of an expansion on a release by a publication such as *The Wall Street Journal* is immeasurably more important to an organization than hundreds of clippings from a variety of non-essential periodicals.

Merchandising the clippings, resulting from a specific news release, is a valuable use of news clippings. As an example, a release on a new product by one's organization, which results in a wide spread of clippings, can be montaged on a broadside and supplied to company sales personnel. These lend confidence to the salesperson and gives him or her ammunition for use in selling accounts or new prospects. These same broadsides can be used as mailing pieces by the marketing department to indicate to retailers a public acceptance of the new product.

Other departments that obviously can use clippings are accounting or financial, for releases to financial and related publications; legal department, for releases in reference to organizations the company might wish to acquire, or on matters relating to court decisions within the industry.

Although maintaining clipping files or books is a boring task in the public relations department, it is a necessary evil, and maintenance should be meticulous.

| Clipping Services | Assigned to | Date/Time Assigned | Date/Time Completed |
|---|---|---|---|
| I. Take advantage of one or more clipping services. | _____ | _____ | _____ |
| II. Consider subscriptions to:<br>1. National overall clipping service.<br>2. Regional or local clipping service.<br>3. Special interest clipping service. | _____ | _____ | _____ |
| III. Arrange for every news release issued by the company to be provided to all clipping services in time for them to alert their readers. | _____ | _____ | _____ |
| IV. Provide all clipping services with detailed and written instructions on what you want clipped and forwarded to you—and when.<br>1. Instruct the clipping service that you are not interested in casual references to your company or product and that written instructions on selection must be adhered to. | _____ | _____ | _____ |
| V. Prepare a distribution list (with adequate bucksheet) for all those who want to see clippings.<br>1. Consider the duplication of clippings and their routing to pertinent persons on a regular basis.<br>2. Consider a selection of clippings on specific subjects and events to make it a montage mailing piece for retailers or salespersons.<br>3. Assign someone the responsibility for collating clippings into categories and keeping them properly filed—perhaps a press book. | _____ | _____ | _____ |
| VI. Advise various division or department heads (research, financial, legal, etc.) of the value of clipping service. | _____ | _____ | _____ |
| VII. Consider obtaining clippings of competitor's products. | _____ | _____ | _____ |

*(continued)*

| **Clipping Services** | **Assigned to** | **Date/Time Assigned** | **Date/Time Completed** |
|---|---|---|---|
| VIII. Consider obtaining clippings about companies you may acquire, merge with, or be acquired by as to:<br>1. Financial status.<br>2. Industry status.<br>3. Personnel.<br>4. Product lines.<br>5. General acceptability. | _____ | _____ | _____ |
| IX. Supply your sales and/or marketing department with clippings relating to principal accounts, customers, or distributors.<br>1. Consider clippings on prospective customers.<br>2. Consider clippings on prospective wholesalers or dealers. | _____ | _____ | _____ |
| X. Conduct a clipping service audit:<br>1. Recognize that no clipping service can average more than 35 percent of all returns on all news releases.<br>2. Check on the requirement that the clipping service is to provide you with special responses relating to special releases.<br>3. Require the clipping service to indicate to you how successful certain types of releases are.<br>4. Require the clipping service to advise you as to which media will accept photographs, artwork, foreign stories, highly technical stories, human interest stories, etc. | _____ | _____ | _____ |
| XI. If desirable, make arrangements with companies to provide videotapes of TV news programs and radio reports of radio programs in transcript form. | _____ | _____ | _____ |

*(continued)*

| Clipping Services | Assigned to | Date/Time Assigned | Date/Time Completed |
|---|---|---|---|
| XII. Decide with the CEO the cost effectiveness ratio of clipping services. Charge to the various departments that part of the service pertaining to them. | _____ | _____ | _____ |
| XIII. Consider relying on your outside PR counsel to operate your clipping service program. | _____ | _____ | _____ |

# 14

# AMBIENT
# PRESS HOSTILITY

It is natural that wherever there is an adversarial relationship between two groups or entities, there will be cries of hostility or antagonism by one or the other, or both. It is imperative that the DPR, and through him or her, the CEO and the senior executives of the organization, analyze the relationship and recognize the adversarial from the antagonistic.

If it is determined that the confrontation is one actually of two adversaries, every effort must be exerted to maintain it in a civil manner. It is a perfectly normal relationship between news media and the organizations and groups within their milieu.

If, however, it has eroded into an open hostility, the DPR must assess its dimension and determine its origin with the goal of bringing the relationship back to the norm.

The importance of determining the origin of the hostility cannot be over-emphasized. In many cases, an antagonism which seems historical and organization-wide, can be traced to a single individual with an over-developed sense of injury, frustration, or personal pique. On the other hand, there are cases where an active hostility is the result of a corporate policy or attitude, also deriving from an individual.

In either case, it is the obligation of the DPR to resolve the problem and, given agreement, willingness and time to get the situation to a level of operating civility.

It is unfortunate that there seems to be a new and arrogant attitude on the part of some corporate officers at the highest levels. Obviously, this filters down to the lower levels of management and the result is a response to news media inquiries of, "The hell with them. Give them nothing. What can they do to us?"

These few deliberate provocations should not be allowed to become the norm. No CEO thinking of long-term benefit for his or her organization can believe that "they" can have no effect. Instead, the CEO can capitalize on a working relationship to the short-term and long-term advantage to his or her organization.

If the original error or misunderstanding was on the part of the organization or any person in it, the DPR should begin a campaign to correct the company's policy or actions. If it is the fault of the news medium, he or she must meet with the pertinent persons and bring everything out into the open. Only then can both parties reach an agreeable working relationship.

| Ambient Press Hostility | Assigned to | Date/Time Assigned | Date/Time Completed |
|---|---|---|---|
| I. Compile, over a sixty-day period, in headquarters, plant, facility, or community: | _____ | _____ | _____ |
|   1. All new stories about organization. | | | |
|   2. References to your organization in other stories. | | | |
|   3. Record of telephone inquiries by news media. | | | |
|   4. Record of number of personal meetings with both print and electronic media. | | | |
|   5. Record of TV/radio interviews, panel shows, etc., by company personnel. | | | |
|   6. Record of taped or live quotations about the company. | | | |
| II. Compile during the same time period and areas an assessment of news media attitudes toward your organization by: | _____ | _____ | _____ |
|   a. Your executives. | | | |
|   b. Your PR staff. | | | |
|   c. Any employees. | | | |
|   d. Community leaders (except those in media). | | | |
| III. Compile in the same period and areas: | _____ | _____ | _____ |
|   1. A list of all media requests: | | | |
|     a. Personal. | | | |
|     b. Written. | | | |
|     c. Telephone. | | | |
|   2. List of completed responses and satisfactory answers. | | | |
|   3. List of uncompleted responses to inquiries or requests—with list of reasons for failure to satisfy. | | | |
| IV. Determine a "bottom line" attitude as a result of the above lists. | _____ | _____ | _____ |
|   1. Evaluate attitudes on the part of the media. | | | |

*(continued)*

| Ambient Press Hostility | Assigned to | Date/Time Assigned | Date/Time Completed |
|---|---|---|---|
| 2. Make an honest and factual determination whether it is: | | | |
|   a. Real or imagined hostility. | | | |
|   b. Normal adversary relationship. | | | |
|   c. Personality situations. | | | |
|   d. Common to all contacts. | | | |
| 3. Try to isolate one or more causes and determine if they are: | | | |
|   a. The fault of the company. | | | |
|   b. The fault of company procedures in responding to requests. | | | |
|   c. Single incident cause. | | | |
|   d. The result of a series of organization's actions. | | | |
|   e. Historical or traditional. | | | |
|   f. Deliberate policy by one medium which has been effective and is consequently followed by other media. | | | |
| V. Determine corrective measures to be attempted: | _____ | _____ | _____ |
| 1. Correction and implementation of response procedure to media requests or inquiries | | | |
| 2. Evaluate strategy and methodology of corrective approach to media: | | | |
|   a. Time, gradual, and soft-sell. | | | |
|   b. Bold, direct confrontation to clear the air and reach a working relationship agreeable to both media and your company and its personnel. | | | |
|   c. Disregard and live with it. | | | |
|   d. Hard-nosed attitude and defiance. | | | |
| 3. If the decision is to work out some plan of a positive relationship: | | | |
|   a. Visit each news medium and meet with executives and pertinent individuals; explain your desire to establish a working procedure agreeable to company and media. | | | |

*(continued)*

| | Ambient Press Hostility | Assigned to | Date/Time Assigned | Date/Time Completed |
|---|---|---|---|---|
| b. | Invite individual media and its people to a business lunch where relevant matters can be thrashed out. | | | |
| c. | Have successive meetings with each media representative as quickly as possible. | | | |
| d. | Invite complaints at these meetings. | | | |
| e. | State company complaints. | | | |
| f. | Set up mutually agreeable ground rules. | | | |
| g. | Stick by rules and insist that media people follow suit. | | | |

# Can a corporation speak its mind in public?

Not long ago, the Supreme Court ruled that corporations are entitled to the right of free speech.

However, when Kaiser Aluminum & Chemical Corporation tried to exercise this right recently, it was denied by the three major television networks.

Our idea was to produce three commercials drawing attention to issues we felt were of major concern to the people of America. One was about energy. The others dealt with free enterprise, and governmental red tape. (The commercials are shown below). We believed at the time that we were exercising our right to speak our mind. We were willing to pay for the air time to run these commercials. And we clearly identified these messages as opinions of our company.

But when we submitted them to the networks, the commercials were rejected. The networks said they would refuse to air them. Not because they were untrue, misleading, or in any way inaccurate. But simply because they were controversial or not acceptable material.

One network cited the "Fairness Doctrine" as a reason for rejecting the commercials. This doctrine was formulated by the Federal Communications Commission (FCC) to insure that a fair balance of opinion is presented on television. We believe, too, that television should present a fair balance of opinion. Even ours.

There is no doubt that television is one of the most powerful media in operation today. And we believe that access to this medium must be kept free and open.

*If you believe a free exchange of ideas is as important now as it's ever been, write your elected representatives or write us at Kaiser Aluminum. Room #776 KB. 300 Lakeside Drive, Oakland, California 94643. Let your voice be heard.*

**Announcer**
Is free enterprise an endangered species? How much government regulation is enough? Is business bad just because it's big? Or does a country like ours require a diversity of business—both big and small?

Will excessive control over big business lead to control over all our business?

The answers are up to you.

Whatever your views let your elected representatives know.

People, one by one, need to speak up now. You can help keep free enterprise free.

A message from Kaiser Aluminum.
One person can make a difference.

**Announcer**
Some people are calling the energy crisis a hoax. Others say that at the rate we're using up our oil reserves we'll be down to our last drop in our children's lifetime.

Whoever's right, one thing is clear. America needs an energy plan for the future *now.* One that uses all resources available from coal and nuclear power to solar.

But we're only going to get it if people, one by one, demand it.

Whatever your views, let your elected representatives know now.

There's not much we can do when the light goes out.

A message from Kaiser Aluminum.
One person can make a difference.

**Official Voices (Overlapping)**
Applications should be filled out in triplicate...
Forms should be returned by the 19th or penalty charges...
The Bureau requires all permits to...
The Department must be notified...
Send one copy to...

**Announcer**
It's red tape. In 1977, America spent $100 billion on federal paperwork alone. And in the end we *all* pay for it.

But if people, one by one, start speaking out, we can begin untangling America's knottiest problem.

A message from Kaiser Aluminum.
One person can make a difference.

# IV

# CONSUMER AFFAIRS

Helping a company to make a profit and stay in business is the reason consumer affairs is a major public relations function. Anything a public relations practitioner can do to contribute to a company's marketing efforts is highly valued. Added to this objective is a concern for the seller-buyer relationship which the consumerism movement represents.

**PRODUCT PUBLICITY** Through product publicity, public relations contributes to a company's total "marketing mix." The other ingredients are advertising, promotion, and personal selling. Each plays a part in the marketing process—the selling and distribution of a company's products and services. Product publicity contributes by:

> ► Attracting favorable attention to a product in the mass media and specialized media.
> ► Creating a climate of opinion in which advertising can be most effective.

► Reaching opinion leaders and product innovators who judge products and influence their rate of adoption.
► Casting the "halo" of the corporate image on products, thus providing product assurance and a loyalty consideration.
► Adding excitement, glamour, and other positive associations to the product.

The purpose of product publicity is not to get "free space" in place of advertising—although that's an argument often used. When a reader or viewer sees a product as a news story, the product receives an implied endorsement by the medium in which it appears. Whatever appealing features may be contained in the news story becomes associated with the product. The product receives "status-conferral" by the media.

If a product is aimed at highly segmented audiences, advertising possibilities may not exist or are uneconomical. In such cases, product publicity is a "rifle" approach to reach those audiences economically and with appeals pertinent to them.

News about a company and institutional advertising build a company's image. So does a company's performance and consumers' experience with its products. The corporate image serves as surrogate information about the seller of the product: the quality, taste, and product stewardship. It is particularly important for new products and is further discussed in that section.

**CONSUMERISM** Dissatisfaction with the seller-buyer relationship is at the root of the consumerism movement. The gap between consumer expectations and product performance became too wide. Expectations rose with higher consumer incomes and education. Advertising claims contributed too. Performance has suffered because of the increasing complexity of some products, entry of new groups of workers with lower skills, and the impersonalization of sales.

Consumerism is not just another of those pesky social problems that divert management attention from more important business problems. Consumerism strikes at the heart of business—producing and marketing the company's products. The problem can't be handled in a quarantine fashion by simply creating a new vice presidency to listen to consumer complaints. There must be feedback to everybody in the company who deals with products. Then there must be corrective action.

Products must be designed to satisfy consumer wants, manufactured to meet acceptable standards, sold to informed customers, and, where relevant, serviced throughout the life of the product. Management's orientation must not be limited to only one point in this process —making the sale—but must be broadened to include the total spectrum of the seller-buyer relationship.

**CONSUMER PROTECTION REGULATION** Before the era of consumerism in the early 1960s, government intervention in the marketplace was chiefly limited to antitrust action to keep competition alive. This would keep prices low and quality high. The Sherman Act of 1890, the Clayton Act of 1914, and the Federal Trade Commission Act of 1914 remain the foundation of this approach.

Secondary legislation dealt with a few specific abuses. For example, Upton Sinclair's graphic depiction of unsavory conditions in the meatpacking industry in his book, *The Jungle,* led to passage of the Food and Drug Act of 1904.

It was President John F. Kennedy's Consumer Bill of Rights statement of 1962 that set the stage for a flood of new legislation. Consumer rights were: to be informed, to be safe, to choose, and to be heard. Many companies echoed these in their consumer policy statements, and added others, such as the right of redress of grievances.

"Caveat emptor"—let the buyer beware—was the unwritten code of the marketplace until the consumerism movement replaced it with "caveat venditor"—let the seller beware. Important among the seller's new obligation is the disclosure of product information. That requirement has also led to more consumer education activity.

**CONSUMER AFFAIRS UNIT** In response to consumerism, many companies established independent consumer affairs departments reporting directly to a senior officer. A smaller proportion of companies have reporting channels to a public relations department head.

Most of the skills, attitudes, and knowledge required for consumer affairs parallel those of public relations. So, whether a consumer affairs unit is an independent department or reports to public relations does not alter the qualifications needed or the principles and practices followed. The key is close coordination between the two. Furthermore, consumer affairs must work closely with all organizational units and top management in order to take corrective action on consumer grievances.

Consumer affairs specialists now have their own organization, the Society of Consumer Affairs Professionals in Business (SOCAP), located at 777 14th Street, NW, Washington, DC 20005.

**ISSUES MANAGEMENT**

Consumerism is one of the major events that opened management's mind to the importance of issues management—better expressed as involvement in the public policy process. To avoid further government regulation, companies and industries are carefully monitoring the socio-political environment. They look for further signs of consumer discontent, statements and activities by consumer advocates, media treatment of consumer news, and signs of legislative intent.

The idea, then, is to intervene as early as possible to resolve an emerging issue. Usually, this requires voluntary action by a company or industry to improve on some aspect of the buyer-seller relationship. For example, companies have:

> ► Improved product service organizations. Also, "tel-tags" at point of purchase, and special listings in telephone books tell consumers how to reach these units.
> ► More informative advertising copy.
> ► Simple-language warranty specifications.
> ► Product safety standards.

Constant evaluation is necessary to know how well consumer affairs efforts address complaints of consumers and issues raised by consumer advocates. As discussed in the following sections, complaints must routinely be analyzed so that basic causes of problems can be corrected. Consumer feedback systems must be improved. Consumers must be given an opportunity to participate in the making of consumer policies. When product deficiencies occur, recall systems must be activated. Many of the specifics are applications of basic public relations principles.

# 15

# CORPORATE ADVERTISING

A scanning of any major newspaper shows that an increasing number of advertisements don't talk exclusively about products; instead they say something about the personality and character of a corporation or industry. The rationale behind such advertising is that people evaluate an organization in order to make certain kinds of decisions about it. That overall evaluation affects people's attitudes toward everything else it says or does.

There is no hard and fast delineation between different kinds of corporate advertising. Besides, the ads often cover several categories, including product advertising. These distinctions, however, are helpful:

- ► Corporate image and identification advertising.
- ► Corporate social responsibility advertising.
- ► Issue or advocacy advertising.

This section treats only the first of these categories. Corporate social responsibility advertising is treated elsewhere as a form of social reporting. Issue or advocacy advertising is treated herein.

**CORPORATE IMAGE** People develop impressions—or images—about companies. These impressions have a life of their own. They may or may not reflect the reality of the company, and they may or may not square with the impressions managers have of their company. Although some practitioners find the term *corporate image* repugnant, it is a reminder that "pictures in the head," as Walter Lippmann put it, must be dealt with.

Three aspects of the corporate image are important:

1. Awareness or familiarity with the company: Have people heard of the company? Do they know anything about it? How much?

2. Liking for the company: Do people have favorable attitudes toward the company? Do they like it a little, or a lot?

3. Distinctive personality traits: What kinds of adjectives do people use to describe the company? Is it cold, unfriendly, conservative? Is it progressive, innovative, successful? Does the company stand out in any respect? Is it unique in any way?

**PUBLICS** The emphasis given to each aspect of the corporate image and the details provided vary with the audience at which corporate advertising is aimed. It pays a company to be well known in the financial community, particularly when new acquisitions or corporate strategies lead to a change in name. The new name and identity must be announced and publicized so that traders will be aware of it. With no other group is awareness of the entire corporate entity as important as it is with the financial community. After all, it is the company as a whole whose stocks and bonds are traded.

Awareness by consumers of the corporate image is important when it is used as the brand designation or a brand-reinforcer. As the section on product boycotts illustrates, some companies may decide on a low profile strategy in favor of creating greater brand awareness. Some companies take the pragmatic approach of advising their subsidiaries or product divisions to link brands and products with the corporate name when it helps, and not to when it doesn't help.

Favorable attitudes toward a company contribute to the total marketing effort. In addition to a company's overall reputation, a high rating in traits related to products and services is important. Customers emphasize the quality, durability, and newness of products and the reasonableness of prices. They may want to know that the company is progressive and is one of the industry leaders in research.

A relatively new dimension in consumer behavior is the company's reputation as a socially responsible corporate citizen. When a choice exists, a small percentage of consumers shun products of a company with a poor environmental record or one that violates some other social expectation. For these consumers, social responsibility advertising may be helpful.

## CORPORATE IDENTIFICATION

Most corporate advertising includes a corporate signature or logotype that symbolizes the company. The design of these corporate symbols and other visual devices that help people quickly and easily to identify an organization falls in the province of corporate identification specialists. They combine a knowledge of public relations with graphic art skills.

The following criteria should be met by corporate identification programs:

- ► Is the "feeling" of the corporation conveyed? Does it identify and express its personality?
- ► Is it unique, memorable, easy to read and pronounce, relatively short, clear, and simple? Does it lend itself for use in logotype?
- ► Is it adaptable to international markets? Is it non-geographical and does it have similar pronunciations in major languages?
- ► Is it suitable as a brand name for a wide range of products?
- ► Does it accurately describe, represent, or even connote the scope of company operations?
- ► Does it have desirable associations and an absence of negative connotations?
- ► Does it create favorable feelings of friendliness and warmth?

| Corporate Advertising | Assigned to | Date/Time Assigned | Date/Time Completed |
|---|---|---|---|
| I. Have top management decide on the use of corporate, institutional, or advocacy advertising as a tool to further company goals. Delineate these goals. | _____ | _____ | _____ |
| II. Provide an adequate budget for corporate advertising. | _____ | _____ | _____ |
| III. Decide whether the same advertising agency should handle corporate as well as product advertising. | _____ | _____ | _____ |
| IV. Decide whether to use corporate advertising exclusively as a means of establishing the company's prestige or as a cachet for:<br>1. Stockholders and investors.<br>2. OEM customers.<br>3. Government. | _____ | _____ | _____ |
| V. Determine which is the most efficacious approach in your organization's advertising:<br>1. Multiple targets.<br>2. Series of single targets. | _____ | _____ | _____ |
| VI. Delineate individual targets or goals sufficiently clearly so they can be expressed succinctly and grammatically. | _____ | _____ | _____ |
| VII. Arrange a meeting with the CEO and executive committee after you have had a meeting with the advertising agency. | _____ | _____ | _____ |
| VIII. Use these criteria in selecting an advertising agency:<br>1. Absence of conflict with other clients.<br>2. Track record of successful work with other clients.<br>3. Satisfaction with agency samples and exhibits. | _____ | _____ | _____ |

*(continued)*

| **Corporate Advertising** | **Assigned to** | **Date/Time Assigned** | **Date/Time Completed** |
|---|---|---|---|
| IX. After selecting an agency, decide whether the campaigns will have a definite period or be on-going "until forbidden." | _____ | _____ | _____ |
| X. Decide whether the following features of dramatic artwork will be included: | _____ | _____ | _____ |
|   1. Dramatic real-life situation photos. | | | |
|     a. Obtain clearances from subjects in photos. | | | |
|     b. Decide on proper fee for photo clearances. | | | |
|     c. Decide on residual uses. | | | |
|   2. Use of "reason why" copy. | | | |
|   3. Use of a series of Q & A's. | | | |
|   4. Use of highly topical and/or controversial matter for copy content. | | | |
|   5. Style of copy: | | | |
|     a. Conversational. | | | |
|     b. Authoritative. | | | |
|     c. Learnedly logical (scholarly). | | | |
|     d. Factual. | | | |
|   6. Arrange for a contingency series of ads for use in case of unexpected breaks. | | | |
|     a. Instruct the advertising media of possible use of contingency ads. | | | |
|     b. Instruct agency on what events trigger use of contingency ads. | | | |
| XI. Ascertain that the proposed corporate advertising will mesh compatibly with all other promotion efforts of the company: | _____ | _____ | _____ |
|   1. Product advertising. | | | |
|   2. Sales promotion program. | | | |
|   3. Existing literature of any kind. | | | |
|   4. PR programs. | | | |
|   5. Publicity campaigns. | | | |
|   6. Canned speeches made by company executives. | | | |

*(continued)*

| **Corporate Advertising** | **Assigned to** | **Date/Time Assigned** | **Date/Time Completed** |
|---|---|---|---|
| XII. After the program is established and first proofs have been approved, arrange for distribution of notice of company's intent, and send copies of proofs to:<br>  1. Employees (bulletin boards).<br>  2. Industry.<br>  3. Vendors.<br>  4. Stockholders.<br>  5. Senators and congressmen or state legislators.<br>  6. Union(s). | _____ | _____ | _____ |
| XIII. Consider the use of plant city news media as an outlet for the campaign. | _____ | _____ | _____ |
| XIV. Decide whether your corporate campaign will carry a request for action.<br>  1. Decide on who will be responsible for responding to letters.<br>  2. Provide readers with a list of names and addresses of those you wish them to communicate with. | _____ | _____ | _____ |
| XV. Request the ad agency to provide the research leading to proper media selection and placement. | _____ | _____ | _____ |

# 16

# ADVERTISING AND PACKAGE CLAIMS

Advertising is an admixture of information and persuasion. Persuasion usually wins out because appeals to a consumer's self-image, pleasant associations with products, and use of superlatives create sales. It's what a product will do for people that counts, not product specification.

**PUFFERY** Persuasion easily leads to puffery. Advertising and other sales representations are made which praise a sales item with vague and general subjective opinions, superlatives, or exaggerations and without stating specific facts. Describing P. T. Barnum's circus as "The Greatest Show on Earth" is a classic. Other old and familiar advertising phrases are: Coca-Cola's "It's the real thing," "You can be sure if it's Westinghouse," "Old Grand Dad—head of the bourbon family," Avis' "We try harder," and AT&T's "Reach Out."

The line between falsity and deception is the crux of the truth-in-advertising problem. Objective facts determine whether a statement is true or false, but deception is based on subjective reactions by consumers.

The Federal Trade Commission accused the makers of Hot Wheels and Johnny Lightning toy racers of deceptive television advertising when the cars were shown moving at high speeds along their tracks. That's what photography from a certain angle realistically portrayed. Still, the FTC thought that the ad, while technically accurate, would deceive children badly. Section 5. (a)(1) of the Federal Trade Commission Act declares unlawful "unfair methods of competition in commerce, and unfair or deceptive acts of practices in commerce. . . . "

Public relations practitioners must keep an eye on any corporate communications, including advertising, that might harm the company's credibility. How is anything the company says to be believed if people consider product claims only partly true or outright deceptive? As with all dimensions of the corporate image, it is the impression people have that counts, not the question of technical accuracy.

**MORE INFORMATION** The consumerism movement demands that companies provide more information about their products and that claims can be substantiated. In large measure, the standards of the Securities and Exchange Commission of "full and timely disclosure" are being applied to the marketplace for products and services. The consumer must be given all the "material facts" that enable him or her to make a rational decision. One measure of what facts are relevant is what the *Consumer's Report* publishes.

An increasing amount of consumer protection legislation and regulation requires companies to provide more information:

> ► Kefauver-Harris Drug Amendments (1962) requires drug manufacturers to label all drugs by generic name.
> ► Fair Packaging and Labeling Act (1966) regulates the packaging and labeling of consumer goods and the establishment of voluntary uniform packaging standards.
> ► Truth-in-Lending Act (1968) requires full disclosure of annual interest rates and other finance charges on consumer loans and credit buying.

**CONSUMER EDUCATION** As products become more sophisticated, product information alone is inadequate. A broader knowledge base is needed to interpret facts. Here's where a number of consumer affairs programs should be considered:

► Product publicity feature stories with enough background to make sense of information.
► School consumer education booklets and films that explain how a product (e.g., a computer) works.
► Consumer buying manuals that explain what to look for in buying food, a car, a house, etc.
► Exhibits and conferences that explain complex products such as computers.
► Adult education courses.

| **Advertising and Package Claims** | **Assigned to** | **Date/Time Assigned** | **Date/Time Completed** |
|---|---|---|---|
| I. Make PR policy absolutely clear to marketing, sales, and administrative personnel:<br>　1. All advertising claims will be irrefutable.<br>　2. There will be no ambiguity about product claims.<br>　3. There will be no "weasel wording" in order to piggy-back on a trend.<br>　4. DPR will see and approve all copy before it is released. | _____ | _____ | _____ |
| II. If celebrity endorsement claims are made in advertising or package copy or promotional literature, they must meet the criteria of being:<br>　1. True.<br>　2. Credible.<br>　3. Substantiable. | _____ | _____ | _____ |
| III. Read all copy to avoid such statements as "all natural product" when followed by reference to artificial color ingredients, etc. | _____ | _____ | _____ |
| IV. If advertising or package copy offers a guarantee or warranty, make certain that it is actually a guarantee or warranty, and that its terms are totally spelled out in legible, basic English.<br>　1. Check on how convenient it is for a consumer to achieve satisfaction of guarantee.<br>　2. Make the dealer fully aware of the guarantee—its terms and dealer participation to provide consumer satisfaction within reasonable time. | _____ | _____ | _____ |
| V. Have your artwork depict your product in such dimensions and proportions that the consumer or purchaser will not be offended or mislead.<br>　1. If pertinent, use the phrase "actual size" under photograph or artwork. | _____ | _____ | _____ |

*(continued)*

| Advertising and Package Claims | Assigned to | Date/Time Assigned | Date/Time Completed |
|---|---|---|---|
| VI. Arrange to provide quick response to consumers to communicate their dissatisfaction or complaints to the company. | _____ | _____ | _____ |
| VII. Have the ad agency, the marketing department, or your own staff check the regulations of the Federal Trade Commission, Postal Service, state codes, and other governmental restrictive requirements. | _____ | _____ | _____ |
| VIII. Assure that product advertising is compatible with corporate advertising and/or promotional material and public relations program. | _____ | _____ | _____ |

# 17

# NEW PRODUCT ANNOUNCEMENTS

Through product publicity, public relations is a vital part of a company's total marketing program. New product announcements allow the greatest scope for product publicity because something new excites the attention of people and is newsworthy.

Competition for people's attention and media acceptance is so great, however, that only the most notable and attractive ideas reach the publicity threshold. Product publicity starts with a clever idea. The focus is on creativity.

Uniqueness is the key to new product announcements. Economists call this feature product differentiation. What sets your product apart from others? In searching for this idea, attention should be given not only to product characteristics but to how they relate to consumer needs. That's the real secret of marketing. It's also the way news releases can play up the human angle which enhances media acceptability.

**MEDIA RELATIONS** In addition to the use of general media, there is a need for product publicity aimed at specific segments—those consumers most likely to need and want a product. The more a publicist knows about the specific readers and viewers reached by different print and electronic media, the more effective his or her campaign will be.

There are almost 2000 consumer magazines, most of which reach people with particular interests in fishing, hunting, country farming, cooking, recreation vehicles, home computers, etc. Virtually every business and occupation is represented by almost 4000 trade publications. *Bacon's Publicity Checker* lists most of these special-interest publications and the names of editors who cover specific subjects.

Special events attract media attention, especially that of the broadcast media that flourish on visual material. Product publicity then becomes part of the news. The same results can be achieved through good timing—by associating a product with a regular news event.

**DEALER RELATIONS** New products must be introduced, and usually explained, to dealers who will handle them. Special brochures, sales literature, and newsletters are useful vehicles. When a product is so different from previous ones that much explanation and demonstration is needed, audio-visual techniques are necessary. Video cassettes, video discs, or live closed-circuit or cable television are excellent instruments. In live situations, dealers should be given an opportunity to ask questions—either by a phone hookup, or through the growing use of interactive TV.

| New Product Announcements | Assigned to | Date/Time Assigned | Date/Time Completed |
|---|---|---|---|
| I. Explore with the marketing vice president the possible uses, outlets, targets for media determinants for advertising, promotion, and publicity. | _____ | _____ | _____ |
| II. Meet with marketing vice president, product manager, and advertising director to determine product slants and their relationship to company goods, other product lines, and competing products. | _____ | _____ | _____ |
| III. Inspect and approve packaging before completion. Package size must not be misleading. | _____ | _____ | _____ |
| IV. Prior to any campaign launching a new product, study the market research, demographic research, company goals for the product, and the competition. | _____ | _____ | _____ |
| V. Decide appropriate launch data and review.<br>  1. Promotional requirements (test market).<br>  2. Budget details for launch. | _____ | _____ | _____ |
| VI. Set up press conference for first formal announcement.<br>  1. Provide samples for press.<br>  2. Issue release, pictures, and samples to:<br>    a. Trade publications.<br>    b. Pertinent editors of newspapers.<br>    c. Plant community news media.<br>    d. Special interest syndicated columns and writers.<br>    e. TV and radio program personalities.<br>  3. Arrange dealer promotional participation (special displays, local exhibits, local press conference).<br>  4. Get advertising agency to establish co-operative advertising program with market dailies in area. | _____ | _____ | _____ |

*(continued)*

| New Product Announcements | Assigned to | Date/Time Assigned | Date/Time Completed |
|---|---|---|---|
| 5. Arrange "dog and pony" show interviews on local, regional, and national media. | | | |
| 6. Arrange TV tie-ins where applicable. | | | |
| VII. Consider potential for street or mail copy on sampling if applicable. | —— | —— | —— |
| VIII. Consider major national contest featuring product name or use. | —— | —— | —— |
| 1. Tie dealers into contest. | | | |
| 2. Budget for contest advertising program. | | | |
| 3. Schedule a contest publicity campaign. | | | |

# 18

# CONSUMER FEEDBACK AND PARTICIPATION

Consumers' rights to be heard must be accommodated by a company's consumer affairs department. When it isn't, consumer groups, the media, and government on all levels will take up the cudgel for them.

**OUTSIDE CHANNELS** About 100 national consumer organizations and between 500 and 600 on the state and local levels represent consumer interests. Their advocacy efforts increasingly result in a demand for legislative reforms.

Most states and large cities have consumer affairs directors to listen to their consumer constituencies. A state may have a separate department of consumer affairs affiliated with the governor's office, or may have a consumer protection division within the office of the attorney general. Some states have decentralized consumer affairs into specific areas such as energy, banking, aging, and agriculture. Similar patterns are found on the county and local levels. The trade association for state, county, and local consumer protection units is the National Association of Consumer Agency Administrators, 1511 K Street, NW, Washington, DC 20005.

Over 400 "action line reporters" serving the print and broadcast media resolve about two million consumer complaints a year, estimates Fraser Associates' *Contacts in Consumers 1980/81* (1800 K Street NW, Washington, DC 20006). Although some are mainly interested in reporting consumer news, their primary role has been to handle complaints.

**COMPANY CHANNELS** To avoid bad publicity and government intervention, business has learned the value of listening to the consumer. Major consumer feedback channels are:

- ► Surveys and comment cards: Consumers are asked to rate a product or service on different aspects of satisfaction or dissatisfaction.
- ► Hot-lines: Consumers with complaints or questions are invited to call a toll-free number to speak directly to company representatives. Frustrated consumers can "cool off" by being able to act immediately on the source of their frustration.
- ► Complaint-handling system: Phone calls, letters, and personal appearances about product and service deficiencies or difficulties should be monitored and analyzed so that the causes of complaints based on product design, manufacture, or distribution can be corrected.
- ► Consumer advisory boards: A small group of a company's customers meet with management several times a year to offer constructive recommendations on current and future consumers' policies and plans.
- ► Consumer panels: Consumer activists and spokespersons are invited by a company to present their views to management.
- ► Ombudsmen: Although on a company's payroll, these persons serve as an intermediary between the company and consumers. They hear both sides of every story and advise management on the proper course to follow.

Public relations generalists are mainly interested in identifying consumer attitudes toward the company and reviewing company policies that affect consumers. Consumer advisory boards and panels serve as the best channel for these concerns. Public relations directors should participate on them. For this reason, the checklist concentrates on this consumer participation channel.

| Consumer Feedback and Participation | Assigned to | Date/Time Assigned | Date/Time Completed |
|---|---|---|---|
| I. In order to establish consumer acceptance and feedback, arrange for a consumer advisory panel. | _____ | _____ | _____ |
|   1. Appoint panel representatives from each of demographic groups (ethnic, income, etc.). | | | |
|   2. Choose them from twenty to forty principal market areas. | | | |
|   3. Implement panel at local levels. | | | |
|   4. Supply each panel member with company's story and last annual report. | | | |
|   5. Send personal letter from president thanking person for becoming member, and at end of the year, a thank-you letter from president. | | | |
| II. Have monthly meeting. | _____ | _____ | _____ |
|   1. Submit agenda to panel members for suggestions, criticisms, etc. | | | |
| III. Change panel membership each year. Introduce new pertinent company personnel to each panel. | _____ | _____ | _____ |
| IV. Submit product samples to panel before general introduction, with card (multiple choice) for reaction. | _____ | _____ | _____ |
| V. Three or four times a year, arrange for a "market trend" speaker to appear at a panel luncheon. | _____ | _____ | _____ |
| VI. Test company problem areas at these levels. | _____ | _____ | _____ |
| VII. Send appropriate local publicity (photos and captions) of panel members to hometown news media. | _____ | _____ | _____ |
| VIII. Invite press to attend panel meetings. | _____ | _____ | _____ |
| IX. Once or twice a year, arrange for an audiovisual demonstration of product processes or live subjects. | _____ | _____ | _____ |

*(continued)*

| | Consumer Feedback and Participation | Assigned to | Date/Time Assigned | Date/Time Completed |
|---|---|---|---|---|
| X. | Test out industry trade show and exhibit displays with panels. | _____ | _____ | _____ |
| XI. | Aggressively invite feedback. | _____ | _____ | _____ |
| XII. | Get the highest company manager possible to attend panels once a year. | _____ | _____ | _____ |
| XIII. | Watch for proximity of holidays and take appropriate action, e.g., Valentine's Day. | _____ | _____ | _____ |
| XIV. | Submit annual report and, if pertinent, company magazine. | _____ | _____ | _____ |
| XV. | Welcome comment about company in areas aside from products. | _____ | _____ | _____ |

# 19

# CONVENTIONS AND SALES MEETINGS

The task of organizing large-scale meetings typically falls on public relations. Meetings are essentially temporary communication structures designed to get certain business accomplished. The meeting itself is simply the major event of a string of decisions on programming, scheduling of speakers, logistical arrangements, and announcements. News releases and announcements during the event and post-meeting reports culminate the meeting cycle.

Trade and professional associations rely on the typical annual convention to set goals, decide on major policies, review performance, and participate in program activities. A small staff relative to total membership keeps activities going during the year. These activities are guided by an elected chairperson or president and other officers. Committees and task force chairpersons also participate during the year. But the bulk of trade or professional association members get a chance to meet one another once a year during the annual convention.

Sales meetings serve a similar purpose of allowing a geographically dispersed sales force to meet on regular occasions. Sales goals are announced, new products presented, and marketing strategies discussed. Meetings are also an occasion to present awards, provide entertainment, and whip up a sense of camaraderie among the sales force.

As the checklist shows, much advanced planning and attention to minute details are required.

| Conventions and Sales Meetings | Assigned to | Date/Time Assigned | Date/Time Completed |
|---|---|---|---|
| I. Consider each item pertinent to your event. | _____ | _____ | _____ |
| II. Site: | _____ | _____ | _____ |
|    1. Accessibility. | | | |
|    2. Public transportation. | | | |
|    3. Parking. | | | |
|    4. Neighborhood. | | | |
| III. Building: | _____ | _____ | _____ |
|    1. Internal ambience. | | | |
|    2. Bedrooms. | | | |
|    3. Air-conditioned. | | | |
|    4. Lobby areas. | | | |
|    5. Breakfast rooms. | | | |
|    6. Cocktail lounges. | | | |
| IV. Meeting rooms: | _____ | _____ | _____ |
|    1. Number needed. | | | |
|    2. Locations. | | | |
|    3. General meeting room or ballroom. | | | |
|    4. Size of meeting room. | | | |
|    5. Seating set up. | | | |
|    6. Head table. | | | |
|    7. Coffee break area. | | | |
|    8. Registration tables. | | | |
|    9. Room noise. | | | |
|   10. Lighting. | | | |
|   11. Controls. | | | |
|   12. Electrical outlets (spiders). | | | |
|   13. Master switch. | | | |
|   14. Room availability (time). | | | |
|   15. Local staff help availability. | | | |
|   16. Recessing time. | | | |
| V. Group session rooms. | _____ | _____ | _____ |
| VI. P.A./Projection: | _____ | _____ | _____ |
|    1. Self-contained. | | | |
|    2. Built in. | | | |

*(continued)*

| Conventions and Sales Meetings | Assigned to | Date/Time Assigned | Date/Time Completed |
|---|---|---|---|
|    3. Portable. | | | |
|    4. Tape recorder tie-in. | | | |
|    5. Lectern mikes. | | | |
|    6. Stand mikes. | | | |
|    7. House engineer availability. | | | |
|    8. Acoustics, reverberation, clarity. | | | |
|    9. Projection room (built-in or portable). | | | |
| VII. Luncheon/dinner room: | _____ | _____ | _____ |
|    1. P.A./Projection. | | | |
|    2. Lighting. | | | |
|    3. Controls. | | | |
|    4. Air conditioning/heat. | | | |
|    5. Seating set-up. | | | |
|    6. Room capacity. | | | |
|    7. Tables (size and number). | | | |
|    8. Head table. | | | |
|    9. Place settings. | | | |
|   10. Lectern. | | | |
|   11. Number of waiters. | | | |
|   12. Person in charge. | | | |
| VIII. Receptions/Breaks: | _____ | _____ | _____ |
|    1. Private bar. | | | |
|    2. Location. | | | |
|    3. How paid? By drink or by opened bottles. | | | |
|    4. Hors d'oeuvres—canapes. | | | |
|    5. Honored guests separate. | | | |
|    6. Bar closing times and signals. | | | |
|    7. Meal times and signals. | | | |
|    8. Head table signal. | | | |
|    9. Menu selection. | | | |
|   10. Friday or optional choices. | | | |
|   11. Number at head table. | | | |
|   12. Number at each of other tables. | | | |
|   13. Press table. | | | |
|   14. Price guarantee. | | | |

*(continued)*

| | Conventions and Sales Meetings | Assigned to | Date/Time Assigned | Date/Time Completed |
|---|---|---|---|---|
| | 15. Tips and taxes. | | | |
| | 16. Number of waiters. | | | |
| | 17. Kitchen location/service entrance. | | | |
| | 18. Person in charge. | | | |
| IX. | Special Arrangements: | —— | —— | —— |
| | 1. Place cards. | | | |
| | 2. Flowers for head table, others. | | | |
| | 3. Commercial souvenirs. | | | |
| | 4. Movie projector—sound or silent with speaker. | | | |
| | 5. Remote controls. | | | |
| | 6. Tape recorders. | | | |
| | 7. Spare parts. | | | |
| | 8. Extension speakers. | | | |
| | 9. Easels. | | | |
| | 10. Blackboard, flannel board. | | | |
| | 11. Extension cords. | | | |
| | 12. Portable screens. | | | |
| | 13. Podium lights. | | | |
| | 14. Proper circuitry. | | | |
| | 15. Spiders. | | | |
| | 16. Screen. | | | |
| X. | Billing/Checking out: | —— | —— | —— |
| | 1. Firm billing arrangements. | | | |
| | 2. Written agreement on guests charged items. | | | |
| | 3. Charge privileges for host personnel. | | | |
| | 4. Photographer. | | | |
| | 5. Easel lobby signs. | | | |
| | 6. Announcement boards in lobby and elevators. | | | |
| | 7. Speaker introduction. | | | |
| | 8. Timetable. | | | |
| | 9. Head table seating list. | | | |
| | 10. Special VIP invitations and letters. | | | |

*(continued)*

| Conventions and Sales Meetings | Assigned to | Date/Time Assigned | Date/Time Completed |
|---|---|---|---|
| XII. Publicity: | ———— | ———— | ———— |
|  1. Advance release. | | | |
|  2. Advance on major speeches. | | | |
|  3. Copies of speech texts. (See Press Kit Checklist.) | | | |
|  4. Press room location. (See Press Room Checklist.) | | | |
|  5. Typewriters, copy and carbon paper, advance and timely releases, telephones, copying machines, coffee. | | | |
|  6. News conference for major speakers. | | | |
|  7. TV, radio, photography and feature opportunities. | | | |
|  8. Follow-up news releases on meeting. | | | |
|  9. Hometown coverage on attendees. | | | |
|  10. Press room chief. | | | |
| XIII. Staff: Assignments | ———— | ———— | ———— |
|  1. Projection equipment, films, tape recorders. | | | |
|  2. Lights, controls. | | | |
|  3. Liaison with hotel management. | | | |
|  4. VIP adjutant. | | | |
|  5. Assignment list to all hands. | | | |
|  6. Alternates. | | | |
|  7. Staff personnel run through. | | | |
|  8. Security guard for drunks, hecklers, etc. | | | |
| XIV. VIP treatment: | ———— | ———— | ———— |
|  1. VIP transportation to and from city. | | | |
|  2. Arrival/departure time and places. | | | |
|  3. Cars for them—rentals? | | | |
|  4. Rooms and miscellaneous charges. | | | |
|  5. Honorariums. | | | |
|  6. VIP spouses' charges and other costs. | | | |

# 20

# PRODUCT RECALLS

Product recalls are commonplace in modern, industrial societies with their proliferation of consumer products. Many are complex, both in their manufacture and in the sophistication needed for their use. We have all seen newspaper articles or heard television reports about recalls of defective autos, cereals with metal particles, unsafe electrical appliances and toys, and tampons that may cause death.

The consumerism movement is most dramatically and expensively expressed by product recalls. A long list of government agencies—old ones like the Federal Trade Commission and Federal Drug Administration, and new ones like the Consumer Product Safety Commission—are empowered to protect the consumer. The CPSC, for example, can order a manufacturer, wholesaler, distributor, or retailer to recall, repair, or replace any product it deems "unreasonably" risky. It can also seize or ban a product. Thus, it has a life-or-death say over thousands of products. Its technicians and lawyers have poked into a wide range of products: aerosol spray cans, television sets, bicycles, mowers and garden tractors, aluminum home wiring, lamps, ranges, and ovens.

Product recalls are costly in many ways:

> ► Recall communications may require expensive advertising. For example, the manufacturer of a "trouble light," which electrocuted an Air Force captain, was requested by the CPSC to issue warnings through paid prime-time TV 30-seconds spots on each network for three consecutive nights, plus three inserts of 200-line ads in newspapers acounting for 85 percent of circulation. The cost was estimated at half-a-million dollars.
>
> ► "Trial by press release" hurts the reputation of a manufacturer. Government agencies typically use a "goldfish bowl" approach by issuing news releases before sufficient evidence is gathered. The Federal Trade Commission, for example, feels it has "an obligation to give wide dissemination to all Commission actions as they are placed on the public record." The media are all too willing to oblige. Businessmen have complained that neither the FTC nor the media take specific steps to avoid the presumption of guilt.
>
> ► Product liability may ensue. Ford's Pinto case shows how unpredictably expensive jury awards can be. Deaths were caused when the fuel tank of a 1972 Pinto burst into flames during a rear-end collision. The ensuing trial resulted in 125 million dollars in punitive damages.

**PR RULE** Because product recall communications are complicated, public relations practitioners have played a critical role. Many other managers, however, are affected; sales, distribution, packaging, quality control, customer services, and legal counsel. Also affected are advertising managers, designers, and manufacturing and research development workers. Close coordination among all of them is required.

Murphy's Law applies to recall communications: If anything can go wrong, it will. When Corning Glass recalled some of its electric percolators, they learned the value of pre-testing messages. The term *bowl,* which was used to describe the base of its percolator, was misunderstood by people. They saw it as something in which cereal, salad, or soup was placed. So they changed to the popular word *pot* instead.

Corning Glass also applied an important principle of product recalls. All the communication and publicity tools normally used to promote a product should be used to make consumers aware of the recall. Here's what they did:

> ► Retailers were sent counter display packets.
> ► News releases were sent to major networks, wire services, metropolitan and suburban newspapers, radio stations, and TV outlets.
> ► Personal letters were sent to Action Line or "Help" column writers.
> ► Mat releases were sent to suburban papers.
> ► A disc from a popular New York radio station was distributed to stations that normally use their service.
> ► Newspaper ads were run five times in 400 papers nationwide, and 1/3-page ads were run in *Women's Day* magazine.

**PRODUCT STEWARDSHIP** Some companies fear that widespread disclosure and publicity of product defects may be harmful to their reputations. Procter and Gamble would say otherwise. By acting swiftly after their tampon, Rely, was linked with toxic-shock syndrome, it won praise from the public and the Federal Drug Administration. Procter and Gamble management realized that continuing bad publicity about Rely could tarnish all of its other brands, which include Pampers diapers, Tide detergent, Ivory soap, and Crest toothpaste.

A good reputation for product safety and reliability is an essential ingredient of a company's sales efforts. Handling product recall professionally safeguards that valuable asset.

| Product Recalls | Assigned to | Date/Time Assigned | Date/Time Completed |
|---|---|---|---|
| I. A general statement issued to widest possible publicity distribution and practical advertising campaigns for:<br>　1. Trade and consumer publications, electronic media, and consumer advocates.<br>　2. Specify identifiable product series and effects.<br>　3. Spell out steps for implementation of recall.<br>　4. Spell out steps taken to prevent recurrence. | _____ | _____ | _____ |
| II. Immediately send copy of news release and procedure to all distributors and dealers. | _____ | _____ | _____ |
| III. Another news release (same distribution as item I) on methods and procedures for modification, repair, or replacement.<br>　1. Keep it simple and "idiot-proof."<br>　2. Upon receipt of shipped products, prepare and mail acknowledgment cards with date of return shipment specified.<br>　3. In case of nonshippable products, detail procedure in contacting local dealer or distributor. | _____ | _____ | _____ |
| IV. Provide dealer with postage pre-paid acknowledgment cards for customer and manufacturer.<br>　1. Provide dealer with necessary parts and instructions gratis to him or her so it is gratis to customer.<br>　2. Arrange satisfactory labor charge for repairs with dealer to encourage him or her to offer the services to customers. | _____ | _____ | _____ |
| V. PR department to issue blanket statement showing the number of products repaired satisfactorily, and at what cost to the company. | _____ | _____ | _____ |

*(continued)*

| **Product Recalls** | **Assigned to** | **Date/Time Assigned** | **Date/Time Completed** |
|---|---|---|---|
| VI. Keep advertising manager informed. If advertising is required, demand that advertising manager submit copy for PR departmental approval. | _____ | _____ | _____ |
| VII. Follow up on dealers.<br>  1. Check the number of recalled products and the number actually repaired.<br>  2. Send second notice to those who didn't respond.<br>  3. Check media reaction. | _____ | _____ | _____ |

# PRODUCT BOYCOTTS

As a generalized confrontation tactic, the product boycott has been one of the favorites of labor unions, civil rights leaders, consumer groups, and other social activists. It is a form of protest and means of coercion that hits companies in the most vulnerable spot: sales. Consumers are urged by an aggrieved group not to use, buy, or deal with a particular company's products. As a company experiences a drop in sales, it is expected to give in to the demands of the organizing group.

A company is vulnerable to a boycott when these conditions exist:

> ► The grievance used to justify the boycott appeals to the attitudes and values of customers. For example, blacks have conducted boycotts aimed at companies that have not hired enough members of their group.
> ► The mass media publicizes the boycott and customers become aware of it.
> ► The group organizing the boycott is able to communicate directly to consumers through posters, billboards, flyers, and advertisements.

> ► Pickets at retail stores are used as a means of social pressure—and, sometimes, coercion—to "enforce" the boycott.
> ► Customers can afford to cooperate with the boycott because competing or substitute products are available to them.
> ► The company's products are easily identified.

Most of these conditions involve public relations on three levels:

1. A company's marketing and social policies.

2. Its communication strategies.

3. Counter-communications.

**MARKETING AND SOCIAL POLICIES** Consumers are asked to boycott a company's products because of its marketing and social policies. Occasionally, as with meat some years ago, consumers have been urged by consumer groups not to buy a product because its prices have risen too high. The mass media publicizes a particular local boycott, and that news seems to inspire other local groups to do the same. Actually, it is very difficult to organize consumers for such efforts. But public relations efforts must be undertaken to explain the reason for the rise in price and to counter unfounded accusations of profit-gouging.

Not the price, but marketing practices may be the cause of a boycott. For example, church and other groups organized a boycott against the Nestle Company. The grievance was not with this United States-based company, but with its Swiss parent. It was accused of harmful advertising and marketing of its infant formula in third-world countries where economic and sanitary conditions are believed to cause infant malnutrition and deaths.

The public relations function at the policy level is to review the accuracy and legitimacy of the accusations made and to consider the demands of the boycott group. Economic goals are pitted against social responsibility considerations. It is the task of the public relations practitioner to interpret social expectations and anticipate the harm the boycott group could cause. This harm might be in the form of unwanted legislation as well as negative public opinion.

Sometimes a boycott is directed at a seller of a product that buys from companies who are accused of having objectionable labor or social policies. This is a new aspect of "supplier relations" whereby a business firm is asked to judge the morality of its suppliers, or to advance social goals by using the clout of their purchasing power.

This happened when supermarkets were asked by Cesar Chavez's United Farm Workers of America not to sell table grapes grown by California farmers that resisted his demands for higher wages and better working conditions. It also happened when department stores were asked by the Textile Workers Union not to carry J. P. Stevens' goods until the company agreed to bargain collectively with its employees. More recently, boycotts have been inspired by Moral Majority types of religious groups against major advertisers like Procter and Gamble and General Foods, who sponsor sex- and violence-filled television programs.

When a supplier's policies are involved, a seller can argue that it has a higher obligation to the consumer's right of choice. When pressed, some sellers have allowed a boycott group to post information and a boycott request in the store. Because few sellers believe they are in a position to conduct the necessary research to decide on the merits of a particular issue, they typically refuse to cooperate. But they may be faced with these circumstances that change their minds:

- ► Customers in their particular market are "socially conscious."
- ► Items involved account for too small a percentage of sales to jeopardize losing customers.
- ► Pickets are posted and have an impact on sales.
- ► Losses are incurred through use of other tactics, e.g., supermarkets have found abandoned shopping carts fully loaded with groceries—or worse, with fragile products damaged.

**COMMUNICATION STRATEGIES**
Big companies with high profiles are the ones typically targeted by boycott groups. Thus some companies prefer to keep the names of subsidiary companies and particular product brands in the public eye. For example, how many consumers know that Taster's Choice, Quik, Nescafe, Nestea, Decaf, Libbey's and Stouffer's products, Crosse & Blackwell's, etc., have the name "Nestle" on the label?

Companies must therefore carefully consider the broader ramifications of their corporate identification programs. It makes sense to cast the halo of a positive corporate image over all of its products. Consumers have more confidence in what they buy and the financial community recognizes the scope of a company's operations. But the company must equally recognize that such advantages backfire when it is faced with boycott threats.

**COUNTER-**
**COMMUNICATION**

When a boycott is publicized, the company should follow its rumor-handling strategy: Don't inadvertently help in the spread of harmful information. For example, a superchain store would add to its troubles if it took out an institutional or issues ad in a newspaper that covered a broader area than where information about the boycott was already well disseminated. Counter-communication efforts must focus on those groups and neighborhoods already supporting the boycott, or who are at least aware of it.

Product boycotts must always be seen in perspective. They have mainly been used as a tactic by various groups to achieve social goals rather than out of dissatisfaction with a product. Hence this subject must be combined with the two sections on crises and contingency plans. Boycotts are simply a slice of this continuing age of confrontation.

Attention should also be given, however, to the possibilities of negotiations with social action groups and to the establishment of a continuing dialogue with them. The formation of consumer councils is one way to anticipate trouble and work out solutions. Alertness and awareness of areas of vulnerability gives public relations practitioners time to prepare a contingency plan.

| **Product Boycotts** | **Assigned to** | **Date/Time Assigned** | **Date/Time Completed** |
|---|---|---|---|
| I. If product boycott is caused by governmental agency action, check with industry associations to confirm unanimity of statements/positions.<br>  1. If the edict is correct or morally justifiable, take steps to change products and announce immediately. Arrange for immediate and appropriate advertising and publicity.<br>  2. If the edict is incorrect, predict (with industry help) how long the fight will last, and make a proper announcement to expand the advertising and publicity program.<br>  3. In either case, notify the dealer/distributors —after the PR program is implemented. | _____ | _____ | _____ |
| II. If the boycott is political, arrange to meet with:<br>  1. Board chairman.<br>  2. CEO.<br>  3. Senior VPs.<br>  4. Legal counsel.<br>  5. Marketing director.<br>  6. Legislators. | _____ | _____ | _____ |
| III. Evaluate the situation and weigh the pros and cons of either maintaining the status quo or halting the sale of the products entirely or within the regions supporting the boycott. Conduct public opinion survey and editorial survey by telephone or in person.<br>  1. Make the decision.<br>  2. Set up press conference to publicize the decision.<br>  3. Develop advertising campaign to publicize the decision. | _____ | _____ | _____ |
| IV. If the boycott is the result of price opposition, meet with the marketing VP and product manager to determine competetive status. | _____ | _____ | _____ |

*(continued)*

| Product Boycotts | Assigned to | Date/Time Assigned | Date/Time Completed |
|---|---|---|---|
| 1. Change product. | | | |
| 2. Change package. | | | |
| 3. Substitute product. | | | |
| 4. Phase out emphasis. | | | |
| 5. Seek governmental support. | | | |
| V. If the boycott is the result of consumer attitude change toward product lines, advertising claims, or TV posture, check: | ___ | ___ | ___ |
| 1. Industry position and correlate your efforts. | | | |
| 2. Weigh facts for ethical and moral values. | | | |
| 3. Change product, package, or advertising claims. | | | |
| 4. Eliminate products from company lines. | | | |
| 5. Prepare press releases and advertising programs. | | | |
| 6. Check dealer communications. | | | |

# 22

# ADVOCACY ADVERTISING

To compete in the marketplace of ideas, companies have seized upon advocacy, or issue, advertising. It is another form of institutional advertising that promotes the name, character, and personality of an organization.

Advocacy advertising presents a company's ideas and viewpoints on controversial public issues in a public medium. Companies place carefully prepared messages in newspapers, magazines, and—when not in violation of the Fairness Doctrine—the broadcast media. They present facts and arguments that advance the views of a company in opposition to those of government, social adversaries, and the media.

Mobil's ads on the Op-Ed pages of *The New York Times* are among the best known. As stated by Rawleigh Warner, Mobil's chairman:

> . . . we wanted to speak our piece. If we didn't make sense, if we proved not credible over a long period of time, then we would take our lumps. But we wanted to broaden the spectrum of ideas, information and viewpoints, and we were willing to take our chances on the good sense of the people.

Several factors have stimulated the use of advocacy advertising:

► Increasing government regulation of the economy, particularly in the areas of environment, energy, and consumer products.

► Rise in the number and power of the "third sector"—the various public interest and social action groups that seek change in public and corporate policies and are often hostile to business.

► Willingness of the media to publicize criticism of business by various social action groups—and doing so in a "biased" way.

► Growing aggressive stance by corporate management and the recognition that the socio-political environment can have a great impact on the prosperity and survival of the company and the business system.

► Supreme Court decision in First National Bank of Boston vs. Bellotti extending the corporation's rights of free speech to the expression of views on issues beyond those directly related to its business.

Advocacy advertising is a useful and flexible, but limited, tool of public affairs. It provides access to the media with the control that any advertising buys: The exact message written and designed by the company appears in the ad in selected newspapers and other media on the precise dates chosen. There is no intervening gatekeeper, as with news releases, who selects what is news. There is no slanting by editing, excerpting, or placement and space limitations.

This access allows a company to present issues that the media may have neglected or slighted. An issue can therefore be placed on the public agenda. If advocacy advertising accomplishes nothing else, it has the ability to use the power of the mass media to make the public aware of those facts, arguments, and views of interest to a company. It can also create greater understanding of an issue—in the belief that sounder decisions will result.

When it is believed that the media is out of line, advocacy advertising is a means of "setting the record straight." Ads pointing out errors in a reporter's or commentator's story can serve as a powerful corrective force. As stated by Herbert Schmertz, Mobil's vice president of public affairs:

> . . . the advertising is designed to caution aggressive opposition that they do not have the information arena to themselves. If they swing, somebody is going to swing back. This does not stop an opponent, but it makes him careful about making sure of his facts. That is all we ask.

But don't expect advocacy advertising to change attitudes. An ad—or for that matter the mass media as a whole—are only a part of the total influences that mold attitudes and beliefs. Remember that there is a difference between selling a product and selling an idea. Controversy seldom surrounds a product, but by definition, it usually accompanies a public issue.

Product advertising draws on existing motivations and attitudes by simply "canalizing" a consumer's preference for a particular brand. The selling of an idea, however, often runs into opposing attitudes and beliefs, occasionally deep-seated ones. Sometimes the reverse problem occurs: The public is apathetic and unmotivated to burden themselves with issues.

| Advocacy Advertising | Assigned to | Date/Time Assigned | Date/Time Completed |
|---|---|---|---|
| I. Consider advocacy advertising when faced with these situations:<br>　1. To gain access to the mass media on controversial issues.<br>　2. To clarify an issue on which the company has been misunderstood.<br>　3. To publically point out errors or bias in media reporting.<br>　4. To promote the free enterprise system. | _____ | _____ | _____ |
| II. Identify the type of audience you want to reach:<br>　1. Congressmen or legislative blocs.<br>　2. Other public officials.<br>　3. Opinion leaders.<br>　4. Knowledgeable public.<br>　5. General public. | _____ | _____ | _____ |
| III. Be realistic in what advocacy advertising can accomplish:<br>　1. To draw attention to an issue.<br>　2. To increase the legitimacy of an issue.<br>　3. To improve understanding of an issue.<br>　4. To warn opponents that company is ready to fight.<br>　5. To influence attitudes.<br>　6. To urge people to take action.<br>　7. To define organization's stance, philosophy, and policies. | _____ | _____ | _____ |
| IV. Prepare advocacy ads that meet these standards:<br>　1. Use rational, well-documented, persuasive arguments. Remember that some audiences you may want to reach are better informed than the average citizen.<br>　2. Be accurate and fair in presenting information. Be prepared to substantiate facts and claims. | _____ | _____ | _____ |

*(continued)*

| Advocacy Advertising | Assigned to | Date/Time Assigned | Date/Time Completed |
|---|---|---|---|
| 3. Use independent expert opinion, when possible, to discuss complex issues. | | | |
| 4. Identify a statement of a controversial nature as a viewpoint, not as a statement of fact. | | | |
| 5. Relate to the interests and concerns of the intended audience. | | | |
| 6. Create a credible and personal identity for the company. | | | |
| 7. Clearly identify your sponsorship of the message. | | | |
| V. Make advocacy advertising an integral part of the company's total communications program. | _____ | _____ | _____ |
| 1. Establish and maintain a realistic budget to accomplish desired goal(s). | | | |
| 2. Remember that changes and understanding by the public will not be achieved with "one-shot" programs. Advocacy advertising is an ongoing campaign. | | | |

# V

# EMPLOYEE AND LABOR RELATIONS

Employees are being rediscovered as a prime public. The adage, "public relations begins at home," recognizes the special status of employees as members of an organization. They are truly an internal public who have a major commitment to the organization and who are vitally affected by management policies and actions.

From management's viewpoint, employees are a major asset. This asset can appreciate or depreciate in value depending on how employees are treated. Managers and public relations practitioners are drawing on a knowledge of human behavior in order to improve their chances of having a beneficial relationship.

Five developments are heightening awareness of employees as a critical public:

1. Productivity of American business has been tumbling. 1980 was the third consecutive year of productivity declines. Low productivity causes increases in labor costs and, therefore, adds to inflation. Our ability as a nation to compete overseas is

hampered. Although investment in capital goods is the key to increased productivity, employee motivation and willingness to accept change are also important.

2. Public affairs managers have seized upon employees as a "natural constituency" in supporting organizational objectives in the political arena. When it comes to import restrictions (e.g., in the auto and steel industries), environmental regulations, and other public policies affecting job security, employees tend to side with their managements. Even on broader political issues such as deregulation and reductions in corporate income taxes, the majority of American workers have taken a pro-business stance.

3. Employee rights issues have been flaring up and hounding management. The broad question is whether the Bill of Rights should be extended to basic relationships between employees and managers. These relationships involve rights of expression and dissent, fair procedures, privacy, worker participation, and holding outside political beliefs.

4. More workers with "contemporary values" are entering the labor force. Such employees have less loyalty and commitment to an organization, are more concerned with organizational recognition, want to participate in decisions affecting them, and tend to place leisure before work.

5. The status quo with labor unions is breaking. Unions are intensifying efforts to unionize white collar, "knowledge," and public service workers. But managements are becoming adept in fighting off unions and, in some cases, getting rid of unions. The American public is ambivalent. A large majority approves of unions, in principle; but they question their practices. The public is also more concerned about the power of unions than that of other institutions of society. PATCO is a case in point.

These five developments demand more attention by management to employee relations. Employee concerns must become management's concerns through a process of listening to employees and then acting on the findings. Conversely, management must involve employees with its business goals and political concerns. Better two-way communications and employee participation in decision making is the answer.

Occasionally, crisis management is required. Strikes and other labor activities interfere with normal operations. Special employee communications and media relations efforts must be undertaken. The same is true when layoffs occur.

The checklists are, therefore, of two kinds: those that prepare managers to handle crises and those that build a solid structure of employee relations.

# 23

# STRIKES AND
# LABOR ACTIVITIES

Public relations contributes to efforts by the industrial relations department to deal with labor activities and strikes. The involvement of public relations is threefold:

► To reassess the role of employee communications in creating understanding of the company's economic situation and views toward collective bargaining issues.
► To consider the implications of labor activities for the total political relationship of the company to other power structures of society.
► To keep employees and the public informed of the company's position in the event of a strike and possibly accompanying crises.

The role of public relations in industrial relations has expanded as a result of the Taft-Hartley Act provision which gives management the right to discuss union matters with employees as long as no threat is made or reward promised. Section 8 (c) reads:

"The expressing of any views, arguments, or opinion, or the dissemination thereof, whether in written, printed, graphic or visual form, shall not constitute or be evidence of an unfair labor practice under any of the provisions of this Act, if such expression contains no threat of reprisal or promise of benefits."

But the company must remember that its credibility is most vulnerable as it leaves areas where a mutuality of interest between management and its employees exists and enters into an adversarial relationship.

In the long periods between contract negotiations, the temperature of labor relations climbs. If grievances and other dissatisfactions by employees are not aired by means of the employee feedback system and grievance system, they simmer and contaminate the collective bargaining process. If the company has not kept employees informed about its economic situation and prospects, they might make unrealistic bargaining demands. And if the company doesn't give off the right signals about its bargaining stance, employees and the union might consider the company a push-over.

In anticipation of labor negotiations, companies have considered the following subjects for treatment in their employee communications:

▶ Background information and discussion of subjects that serve as the context for specific bargaining issues, e.g., company profits, the role of productivity as a basis for wage increase.

▶ Economic education that tells employees something about the economic realities faced by the company.

▶ Abstract concepts or discussion avoided in preference for talking about company facts. Distributing the annual report, or a version of it, to employees is one way of providing company-specific economic education.

▶ When the union takes a stand on a specific collective bargaining issue or misinforms employees, the company should discuss those specific issues and points with employees.

During labor negotiations, companies should engage in "diplomatic communications." On the one hand, they should not jeopardize the collective bargaining process by discussing issues that should properly remain on the collective bargaining table. But the company should also keep its employees informed about progress. To the extent possible, "joint communiques" are the best form. But that option depends on whether the relationship with the union is generally harmonious or belligerent.

The company must remember that the adversarial climate is at its peak during negotiations. Only the most objective facts must be presented.

Should a strike develop, a form of crisis communications ensues. The company must be prepared to issue special news bulletins to employees. When a critical stage is reached and the company has an urgent message to announce to its employees, a letter by the president sent to employees' homes is often the best vehicle.

The public becomes the silent partner in many strikes and as a result media interest grows. News releases must be prepared that provide factual information and present the company's stand. The aim is to make public opinion work for the company.

When the strike is over and a contract is signed, the job of employee communications is to restore a spirit of cooperation and bury the suspicions created by the adversarial climate. Issues where there is a unity of interest should be stressed.

| Strikes and Labor Activities | Assigned to | Date/Time Assigned | Date/Time Completed |
|---|---|---|---|
| I. Meet with chief executive and directors of industrial relations, personnel relations to discuss and determine press statement as to:<br>1. Demands.<br>2. Offers.<br>3. Contract periods.<br>4. Relationship to industry practices.<br>5. Dates and times of negotiation meetings as well as who will attend. | _____ | _____ | _____ |
| II. Keep abreast of negotiations. Get all the facts. | _____ | _____ | _____ |
| III. Issue statement to all national and local trade, and electronic and print media. | _____ | _____ | _____ |
| IV. Notify:<br>1. Police.<br>2. National Labor Relations Board.<br>3. State Labor Board.<br>4. Industrial Development Board of State.<br>5. Chambers of Commerce.<br>6. Governor.<br>7. Mayor.<br>8. Community leaders. | _____ | _____ | _____ |
| V. Post copy of statement on company bulletin boards. | _____ | _____ | _____ |
| VI. Security head to work closely with police to assure safe passage of employees, merchandise, and vehicles. | _____ | _____ | _____ |
| VII. Be certain that no employee but CEO designee act as spokesman to the press. | _____ | _____ | _____ |
| VIII. Issue update statements immediately to press and employees simultaneously, via bulletin boards. | _____ | _____ | _____ |
| IX. Avoid all personal, provocative, belligerent, or hostile statements in writing, or in speech to the press or other employees or strikers. | _____ | _____ | _____ |

*(continued)*

| Strikes and Labor Activities | Assigned to | Date/Time Assigned | Date/Time Completed |
|---|---|---|---|
| X. State offer in letter signed by president to strikers' homes, explaining the economics of the situation, and include, *e.g.*, that costs cannot be passed on and demands, if consented to, could cost "x" number of jobs because the company becomes non-competitive. | _____ | _____ | _____ |
| XI. Make personal and private assessment of company stand, including recommendation given CEO by industrial relations (IR) director, and if necessary, argue for a compromise on basis of economics and public reaction. | _____ | _____ | _____ |
| XII. If the strike may last long, notify:<br>1. Customers.<br>2. Dealers.<br>3. Vendors.<br>4. OEM's. | _____ | _____ | _____ |
| XIII. Check corporate and product advertising to assess its relevance to strike. | _____ | _____ | _____ |
| XIV. Consider advertising the company's position during a strike under special circumstances:<br>1. When the media do not accurately or fairly represent the company's position.<br>2. When union advertises and misstates facts or your position.<br>3. When community public opinion becomes an important factor in reaching a settlement. | _____ | _____ | _____ |
| XV. Check scheduled speeches by executives. | _____ | _____ | _____ |
| XVI. When negotiations go into arbitration, work with NLRB spokesperson on timing of any news release, and demand to see the copy at least two hours before it is issued to the press. | _____ | _____ | _____ |

*(continued)*

| **Strikes and Labor Activities** | **Assigned to** | **Date/Time Assigned** | **Date/Time Completed** |
|---|---|---|---|
| XVII. When agreement is reached, issue a joint statement by union and IR director after clearance by membership and CEO. <br> 1. Make every effort by management and fellow workers to avoid hostility to those who have been on strike, and are returning to work. | _____ | _____ | _____ |
| XVIII. Follow up with a note of return: "Let's roll up our sleeves and work together and regain what we have lost"—should be issued. <br> 1. Notices on settlement and details to other <br> a. Employees. <br> b. Dealers. <br> c. Stockholders. <br> d. Press. <br> e. SEC analysts. <br> f. Community leaders. | _____ | _____ | _____ |

# 24

# EMPLOYEE COMMUNICATIONS

Communications are an essential component of any effort to build an organization with employees who have a strong sense of commitment. When this commitment exists, employees enjoy greater job satisfaction and the organization benefits from greater productivity. The power of employee communications is that it ties individual members of an organization together to accomplish a common purpose.

Communications brings out the potential in an organization's human resources—just as electricity sparks life into a light bulb. It unites individuals into groups, and groups into larger bodies that get things done. The extent of a communications network defines the outer limits of an organization.

Face-to-face communications between and among managers and employees in every day work is the foundation of any system of employee communications. That is how work assignments are made, how progress is checked, and plans forged. A public relations practitioner must first ascertain the health of these personal communications before he or she appraises the supplementary communications system.

Supplementary communications are the chief responsibility of the public relations department in the majority of large companies. Newsletters, newspapers, magazines, and electronic media comprise what might well be called a miniature mass media system. Virtually all of the media found in communities are replicated in an organization. These media create a sense of community and provide the cement that unifies different groups into a functioning whole.

Public relations practitioners are the writers, editors, and producers of these miniature mass media systems because they draw on the skills of journalism and mass communication.

The basic inventory of employee communications media includes:

- Company newspaper (house organ).
- Company magazine.
- Newsletters.
- Internal television ("private television").
- Public address systems.
- Small group meetings, e.g., departmental.
- Mass meetings, e.g., of all employees at a "jobholders' meeting."
- Bulletin boards and posters.
- Telephone hotlines and dial-a-phone.
- Handbooks and manuals.
- Personal communications, e.g., letters, benefit communications.

Most employee newspapers and newsletters stress personal news and social events: birthdays, weddings, retirements, promotions, bowling clubs, etc. These human interest items increase readership and help create a feeling of belonging among employees.

Company information must also be prominent in employee publications. Plans for growth, new products, new plant equipment, sales, competition, and other business and economic news affecting the company—and hence, its employees—should be reviewed. Problems faced by the company and ways in which employees can help should be discussed honestly. Increasingly such problems include reference to a company's socio-political environment, particularly government regulations. By including broader topics than social events, employee publications can help form a bond between management and its workers.

There is never a vacuum where there should be communications; there is always some form of communication. The first problem facing the public relations director (who is the voice of management in this area) is to determine whether employee communications are good or bad. His or her effectiveness as a conduit between management and its employees is measured by the openess and understanding among the various groups within the organization.

Public relations tools are the director's capabilities and skills as a communicator. The various media he or she uses are the vehicles.

| Employee Communications | Assigned to | Date/Time Assigned | Date/Time Completed |
|---|---|---|---|
| I. Analyze and assess, on a regular basis, the means and areas of communications with employees. | ——— | ——— | ——— |
| II. Evaluate your organization's in-house publication: | ——— | ——— | ——— |

1. Determine advantages/disadvantages of making the paper a company platform or employee exclusive paper.
2. Do a readership survey.
3. Assess distribution system.
4. Make its format competitive with other small publications.
5. Determine the value and effectiveness of a "President's Column."
   - a. Decide on its frequency—periodic or random (need).
   - b. Tone—personal/chatty, formal/informative, etc.
   - c. Initiative or reactive.
   - d. Consistency in style.
   - e. Platform for management position.
6. Determine the editorial slant and keep it consistent.
7. Keep it timely and topical.
8. Maintain a standard of professional writing.
9. Make sure that there are enough professional, attractive photographs and illustrations.
10. Don't worry about making it an award winner; keep it employee-readable.
11. Maintain a proper balance among:
    - a. Employees' personal doings and social events.
    - b. Vehicle for management utterances and corporate news.
    - c. Pure factual and objective reporting.

(continued)

| | Employee Communications | Assigned to | Date/Time Assigned | Date/Time Completed |
|---|---|---|---|---|
| 12. | Determine whether contests or similar gimmicks will increase employee interest. | | | |
| 13. | Keep check of print order and employee numbers ratio. | | | |
| 14. | Budget for a full time staff or editor, reporter/writers, and photographer. | | | |
| 15. | Make an effort to get a volunteer reporter from each division, department, and facility. | | | |
| 16. | Encourage a large and active letters column. | | | |
| 17. | If copies are delivered on company property, check parking lots, restrooms, etc., for throwaways. | | | |
| 18. | Run a "classified ad" page. | | | |
| 19. | Establish a viable "Swap Shop" column. | | | |
| III. | Check on management letters to employees' homes. | ———— | ———— | ———— |
| 1. | Establish a policy of use: | | | |
| | a. Regular. | | | |
| | b. Occasional (need). | | | |
| | c. Frequency. | | | |
| 2. | Make certain that these are not being sent without real need. | | | |
| 3. | Keep them written: | | | |
| | a. Clearly and directly. | | | |
| | b. Without patronizing the recipient. | | | |
| 4. | If they require action on the part of the employee, make it easy to accomplish. | | | |
| 5. | Check for "echoes" or overreactions. | | | |
| 6. | See that they are addressed appropriately to: | | | |
| | a. Employee. | | | |
| | b. Employee's wife or husband. | | | |
| | c. Employee's family. | | | |

*(continued)*

| | Employee Communications | Assigned to | Date/Time Assigned | Date/Time Completed |
|---|---|---|---|---|
| | 7. Ascertain that they are always signed by the CEO or designated senior official. | | | |
| | 8. Be certain that they do not look like form letters. | | | |
| | 9. Avoid the "Dear sir" salutation, by using first and last names, i.e., "Dear Jim Smith." | | | |
| | 10. If the letters are sent on a regular basis, make sure that the schedule is not so frequent as to lessen their effectiveness. | | | |
| IV. | Check up on all office and plant bulletin boards. | _____ | _____ | _____ |
| | 1. Make sure that there are enough to be seen without having employees go searching for them. | | | |
| | 2. Place them in accessible spots—not in corners—where more than one person can read notices at one time. | | | |
| | 3. Assign one staff member who will be responsible for them:<br>a. Posting material.<br>b. Clearing off obsolete material.<br>c. Maintenance and inspection. | | | |
| | 4. Establish duration or cut-off periods for postings. | | | |
| | 5. Keep enough fasteners on hand so that swiping isn't necessary. | | | |
| | 6. Decide whether they should be compartmentalized.<br>a. Company notices.<br>b. Employee/personal.<br>c. Advertisements by employees ("For Sale," etc.). | | | |
| | 7. Maintain a sharp watch for graffiti and obscenity. | | | |

*(continued)*

| **Employee Communications** | **Assigned to** | **Date/Time Assigned** | **Date/Time Completed** |
|---|---|---|---|
| V. Check on "Suggestion Boxes." | _____ | _____ | _____ |
|    1. Evaluate their being attached to or adjacent to bulletin boards. | | | |
|    2. Assign same staff member responsible for bulletin boards to collect the suggestions. | | | |
|    3. Count, interpret, and evaluate numbers and quality of suggestions submitted each week. | | | |
|    4. Establish and budget for an equitable award plan. | | | |
|    5. Give adequate publicity to award winners, appropriate general and trade news media, hometown paper and TV/radio, company paper, bulletin boards, etc. | | | |
| VI. Establish a system, and publicize it to employees, of emergency notifications by preselected TV/radio stations. | _____ | _____ | _____ |
|    a. Assign a staff member to assume full responsibility. | | | |
|    b. Post that person's phone number (on twenty-four-hour basis) at all facilities and offices. | | | |
| VII. Consider use of video cassettes for PA system and cafeterias. | _____ | _____ | _____ |
| VIII. Assess type, frequency, and need for pay envelope inserts. | _____ | _____ | _____ |
| IX. Make your company, divisional, and departmental employee manuals explicit, easy to read, and referrable. | _____ | _____ | _____ |
|    1. Include all obligations of management as well as employee. | | | |
|    2. Spell out all benefits and how they are obtained. | | | |

*(continued)*

| Employee Communications | Assigned to | Date/Time Assigned | Date/Time Completed |
|---|---|---|---|
| 3. Make it loose-leaf format for additions or changes. | | | |
| 4. In front of each individually handed out manual, leave room for immediate supervisor's name and phone number as well as that of the appropriate person in the Personnel Office. | | | |

# 25

# TRAINING PROGRAMS

Preparing people to do their jobs well is a specialized and very practical form of education. When companies change the designation of their personnel department into a department of human resources, they indicate an awareness of the need for employee training. Such companies also refer to this function as investment in human capital and assign great importance to it.

Several factors account for growing interest in employee training:

► Recognition that worker productivity in the United States has been falling and that this trend must be reversed if the United States is to gain and maintain a stable inflation rate and its eminence in world trade.
► Rapid technological change that makes old skills and knowledge obsolete.
► Shift from manufacturing to the service and knowledge industries which require higher levels of skills and knowledge.
► Tendency to treat employees as if they had lifetime tenure.
► Management recognition of its social responsibility to allow employees to achieve their potential.

The development of human resources is a continuous learning process to acquire new skills, knowledge, and attitudes. Some of this process consists of formal lectures, seminars, conferences, and workshops. When the size of the groups is large enough and the company has qualified instructors, it may itself conduct training programs. A company can also decide to hire part-time instructors or to make arrangements with local schools, colleges, and universities. Various tuition-sharing or refund programs encourage employees to avail themselves of community educational opportunities. Companies also pay for attendance and travel expenses to short-term seminars and conferences. Occasionally, a company will pay tuition and living expenses to enable an employee to earn a degree.

An important part of learning takes place in the regular course of work. This may take the form of on-the-job training, both formal and informal. What is often overlooked is that the influence of peer example, work associates, and the organizational environment may have more effect than all training programs.

Public relations practitioners have the opportunity to play a significant role in employee training through their influence on the "culture of the organization." Practitioners have these tools available to them:

- ► Entire panoply of employee communications media: bulletin boards, newspapers, magazines, internal television, flyers, etc. These vehicles can demonstrate management interest in employee training in general and also identify specific training needs, e.g., safety.
- ► Recognition of employees who have successfully completed training programs by "rewarding" them with mention and pictures in employee publications.
- ► Conduct employee corporate image surveys that identify the strengths and weaknesses in the character and personality of the company and its parts.
- ► In cooperation with the human resources department, conduct morale surveys to help determine training needs of a broad organizational nature, e.g., need for supervisory training in human relations.

Attitudes are an important component of any employee training program. Public relations practitioners have a special role to play in developing a culture within an organization that recognizes the value of personal and organizational growth.

| Training Programs | Assigned to | Date/Time Assigned | Date/Time Completed |
|---|---|---|---|
| I. Check personnel department for a training and development program for executives for advancement to senior management. <br>   1. Explore company taking advantage of courses at management schools of local universities available at no cost to executives. <br>   2. Publicize these when and where available. | _____ | _____ | _____ |
| II. Discover what training programs are available for foremen. <br>   1. Explore the American Management Association's system for use by your company. <br>   2. Publicize these when and where available. | _____ | _____ | _____ |
| III. Check personnel or training programs for all employee betterment. <br>   1. Consider free classes during lunch hours—"Cafeteria Classroom"—to enable employees to improve their skills in language, math, and those abilities required in your company. <br>   2. Publicize these when and where available. | _____ | _____ | _____ |
| IV. Establish a scholarship system for children of employees. Publicize it. | _____ | _____ | _____ |
| V. Assess the tuition remission system for employees who go to school at night. Publicize it. | _____ | _____ | _____ |
| VI. Participate in the Merit Scholar program. Capitalize on the PR which is part of the program. | _____ | _____ | _____ |
| VII. Arrange for your company to offer inducements, incentives, and awards for employees at all levels who seek to improve their contribution to the company. Publicize these internally and externally via local hometown media. | _____ | _____ | _____ |

*(continued)*

| **Training Programs** | **Assigned to** | **Date/Time Assigned** | **Date/Time Completed** |
|---|---|---|---|
| VIII. Investigate internship career programs for ambitious high school and college students to spend their summers at the company, and eventually become full-time employees. | ——— | ——— | ——— |
| IX. Keep supervisors properly informed as to the progress of those employees undertaking educational programs. | ——— | ——— | ——— |
| X. Use available statistical data as indicators of training needs:<br>1. Production, output, costs.<br>2. Scrap, spoilage, wastage.<br>3. Absenteeism and tardiness.<br>4. Labor turnover, quits, discharges.<br>5. Complaints and grievances.<br>6. Disciplinary actions. | ——— | ——— | ——— |
| XI. Use employee feedback system as indicators of needed changes. | ——— | ——— | ——— |

# 26

# KEY PERSONNEL CHANGES

Announcements in employee publications and news releases to the media about new employees and promotions are routine. Unfortunately, they are too routine as far as the mass media are concerned. Most news releases about personnel changes simply aren't newsworthy—except to the employee who is the subject of the release.

Employee surveys show that recognition is one of the top needs of an employee. By printing a story in an employee publication, an organization is able to "reward" an employee. He or she receives further recognition when the local community newspaper covers the story. But to expect a national newspaper or major financial or trade publication to be interested in routine personnel changes is unrealistic.

Key personnel changes are an exception. The quality of top management affects the financial community's appraisal of a company. News releases on such changes should be seen as an obligation. The company is supplying a "material fact" of interest to investors.

News releases should try to include corporate image qualities when describing top personnel.

| Key Personnel Changes | Assigned to | Date/Time Assigned | Date/Time Completed |
|---|---|---|---|
| I. Decide, with the help of top management, whether you will publicize the changes to all levels of personnel. | _____ | _____ | _____ |
| II. Send news releases to home townmedia (electronic and print) and to trade publications of everyone down to foreman level. | _____ | _____ | _____ |
| III. Provide a biographical form in concert with the personnel department. Arrange for a company photographer to take photographs if there is an event. | _____ | _____ | _____ |
| IV. Publicize changes ranging from hiring/promotions to lateral transfers and "resignations."<br>  1. Show subject copy before release in each case.<br>  2. Emphasize to employees that the DPR can not guarantee publication of release.<br>  3. Give company publications copy simultaneously wth external publications. | _____ | _____ | _____ |
| V. Allow face-saving for individuals who have "resigned." | _____ | _____ | _____ |
| VI. Obtain full approval and a signed release from the individual. | _____ | _____ | _____ |
| VII. In case of a top management change, also send release to:<br>  1. Financial press.<br>  2. Security analysts. | _____ | _____ | _____ |

# 27

# LAYOFFS

An impending or actual layoff is a crisis to those affected. The "need to know" is high—about why the layoff is necessary, how it could have been averted, and what can now be done.

Management has an obligation to give information to employees, the local community, and others who are affected by the layoff. How well it meets this obligation influences the attitudes and morale of workers who are not laid off and those who may be rehired in the future. It affects community relations and the reputation of the organization. The standing of a company in the financial community is also at stake.

The information needs of different audiences vary. Employees want to know about severance pay, if any, and other benefits. They are interested in the chances of being rehired—and when. If the company undertakes a job relocation or search program, they need information on how to apply.

The business and financial communities want to know whether layoffs are prompted by efficiency moves or whether they presage further economic difficulties. If layoffs are caused by compliance with environmental regulations, then news of layoffs should be linked with public affairs objectives.

A layoff means that everything has to be laid out in the open.

| Layoffs | Assigned to | Date/Time Assigned | Date/Time Completed |
|---|---|---|---|
| I. Announce a potential layoff internally and externally as soon as it becomes known to the company in order to prevent conflagration of rumors. | _____ | _____ | _____ |
| II. Prepare and send a company statement to every employee at home or on job stating reason for company's inability to prevent layoff and what company plans to do to minimize effect on employees. Check that the personnel or industrial relations manager has notified the appropriate labor union(s). | _____ | _____ | _____ |
| III. Consider each employee individually. Company must not approach the layoff in such a manner that employees are just numbers. Each immediate supervisor of those to be laid off must become acquainted with personal situation of those laid off and these facts considered when deciding who stays and who goes. | _____ | _____ | _____ |
| IV. Follow procedures similar to Plant Closing list. | _____ | _____ | _____ |
| V. Do not run recruiting advertisements at time of layoff if there is any possible crossover in job categories. | _____ | _____ | _____ |
| VI. Encourage management to prohibit the wholesale laying off of older and veteran employees in higher salary brackets in order to accommodate desires of divisional managers. Recognize the moral commitment to these employees. | _____ | _____ | _____ |
| VII. Keep community apprised of layoff developments as they occur. | _____ | _____ | _____ |
| VIII. Maintain optimistic note in all cases of possibility of rehiring—if it is practical and feasible—and give dates. | _____ | _____ | _____ |

*(continued)*

| | Layoffs | Assigned to | Date/Time Assigned | Date/Time Completed |
|---|---|---|---|---|
| IX. | Make severance benefits public in a general release and indicate to the local community that the layoff is not a prelude to closing the plant (if indeed that's the case). | _____ | _____ | _____ |
| X. | Keep nothing hidden. There should be no surprises. | _____ | _____ | _____ |

# COMMUNITY
# RELATIONS

Community relations is grassroots public relations. Here is where the concept of interdependence is put to the test, and here is where the company meets people face-to-face. Public relations practitioners who want to interact with people as well as write news releases find community relations an attractive arena of action.

The modern tendency to segment mass audiences into specialized publics and markets is stretched to its fullest on the community level. Banks, utilities, car dealers, department stores, and merchants understand the importance of community relations because their customers are citizens of the communities they serve. Companies with offices and plants in a town or city recognize the community as the recruiting ground for employees. They also regard community relations as an extension of their employee relations efforts.

**INTERDEPENDENCE** A business organization draws on the infrastructure of a community—its roads, water supply, utilities, fire and police protection, schools, hospitals, and other services—to function efficiently. Mining, oil, and other extractive industries know that when they dig and drill in remote areas where no communities exist, they themselves must provide the infrastructure.

Community relations specialists must take and maintain an inventory of community resources and amenities. If the community has an industrial development office, a look at their brochures and ads reveals the community assets considered attractive for new business establishments. The Chamber of Commerce and town or city hall are also ready to help.

It is in business's self-interest to maintain and improve the communities in which it operates. Traditionally, this is done in two ways: taxes and donations. A business looks for a fair tax structure, employee pool, and efficient municipal services. When taxes are too high relative to services received, the "business climate" is called unfavorable and business relocation may be considered. Exercising the principle of corporate citizenship, community relations specialists work for good local government.

Donations are made to keep the non-profit sector—sometimes called the third sector—healthy. The favorite way of doing this is through the local all-inclusive, single drive campaign. Company managers are often asked to volunteer to head such a drive or to at least participate in it. Employee contributions are solicited. Through this and other fund-raising campaigns, social services in a community are maintained and the quality of life in the community enhanced. Corporate contributions also help to build community good will, improve the corporate image, and strengthen a company's political power.

An important community relations function is to develop policies and guidelines for deciding what community efforts to support and by how much. The old, passive, "rule of thumb" approach of waiting to be approached by a community agency and casually deciding on whether and how much to give, is no longer tolerable. Management expects the same kind of rational approach to philanthropy as to any other kind of business decision.

These guidelines for giving should be considered:

► Area practice—give as much as other companies of similar size.
► Number of company employees who live in a community.
► Past company contributions.
► Community corporate quotas.
► Cost/effectiveness: highest return per dollar of contribution.
► Social services and cultural and recreational facilities used by employees.

Increasingly, companies are contributing services as well as funds to communities. A company may encourage its financial manager to volunteer for duty on a town finance committee, or an engineer or scientist to participate in a science course at a local school. Facilities may also be made available. Banks lend rooms to community organizations.

**URBAN AFFAIRS** The expansion of community relations into urban affairs has accelerated the trend toward greater company involvement in the community. In one sense, the term *urban affairs* simply recognizes the aggregation of small communities into cities and cities into larger megalopolies. Demographic shifts since World War II and at least through the 1960s have been from farms and small towns to metropolitan areas. Increasingly, the United States became urbanized. In 1979 only 32 percent of Americans lived in non-metropolitan areas.

With population concentrations, problems multiply at a rapid rate. Cities have become centers of poverty and collections of minorities with their special problems. Crowding has caused housing shortages, traffic snarls, and pollution. Drug abuse and crime mounted. In response, wealthier residents migrated to the suburbs and beyond, leaving the inner city with fewer resources to draw upon. Corporate headquarters were also attracted to the suburbs.

Race riots and fires in the 1960s brought urban affairs to the attention of top management. Society's social problems became business's problems. The social expectations grew that it was the responsibility of business to help cities solve their social problems.

Urban affairs specialists are advised by their managements to be selective in the social problems the company chooses to tackle. George Champion, former chairman of The Chase Manhattan Bank, said: "Individual businesses would be well-advised to focus on one or two problems to which they could bring special expertise, rather than to spread themselves so thin that the impact would be negligible." Other guidelines followed:

- ► Use objective criteria for spending of corporate dollars.
- ► Concentrate on the company's talents and resources.
- ► Get involved in what the company understands.
- ► Select problems that have an impact on company operations.
- ► Don't just give to established causes; find new, even controversial ones.

A wide variety of urban affairs/community relations programs have been devised to help solve social problems. Their key characteristic is that they deal with specific segments of society and the problems they face:

- ► Special training program for youth drop-outs.
- ► Business indoctrination for neophyte black business people.
- ► Rehabiliation of inner city neighborhoods.
- ► Opening plants in ghettos to create jobs.
- ► Providing child care centers for working mothers.
- ► Establishing "summer interns" to help the hardcore unemployed adjust to work conditions.
- ► Sponsoring summer cultural and recreational programs to keep youths off the streets.

As an increasing number of cities follow the pattern of New York City and run into financing difficulties, pressure on companies to fill the gap of providing services will grow. It is easy to see how urban affairs has merged with public affairs. Business must get involved with government so that it will not inherit an increasing number of social problems by default.

## GRASSROOTS COMMUNICATIONS

The big communications opportunity on the community level is to reach people on a grassroots level. Localized news releases are one means. Many "hometown" stories about company personnel are welcomed by the local daily and weekly newspapers. Local radio and television stations give greater coverage than national networks to business news from companies headquartered in their communities. Such local stories sometimes are picked up by the national media.

More important than reaching the mass media is the opportunity for personal communication. Communication theorists agree that personal influence is by far superior to mass communication as a way of affecting people's attitudes toward business and politics. Thus if a company can use the power of face-to-face communications to persuade their employees and community neighbors to believe in a company's position on an issue of importance to it, then it has gained political muscle. Called grassroots lobbying, these community level communication efforts have greatly contributed to company public affairs campaigns. Congressmen, state officials, and local politicians recognize that votes are the bottom line: what their constituents think counts.

# 28

# PREPARING FOR A NEW PLANT

When an organization constructs or opens a new plant or facility in a community, a process of social change and accommodation is begun that holds important opportunities—and possible problems—for both the organization and the community. The significance of the impact depends, of course, on the size of the facility relative to the size of the community and whether the community has previously experienced such growth.

**SOCIAL BENEFITS AND COSTS** Some individuals and groups in a community usually welcome growth while others become apprehensive. Part of the community's reaction depends on what the perceived benefits and costs are. Therefore, an organization must prepare a kind of economic and social impact statement that lists the pluses and honestly talks about the negatives and what it is doing to minimize them. Some of the typical or possible benefits and costs are:

Benefits
► New jobs.
► New payroll adds to community purchasing power.
► New tax source.

▶ Local purchases by the organization.
▶ Attractive buildings and landscaping.
▶ New community resources, e.g., professional manpower.

Costs
▶ Increased traffic.
▶ Need to expand schools and other community services.
▶ Pollution.
▶ Unwanted types of residents.

When zoning ordinance changes or other requests must first be approved by a community before an organization can plan to move into it, a form of negotiations takes place. The community searches for ways of reducing or eliminating the social costs while trying to increase the social benefits. Often, an organization can make reasonable concessions. For example, the Air Force avoided flights on Sundays during church hours, and a manufacturing plant staggered its working hours to ease the flow of traffic. Even after a facility is established, new problems are worked out with the community.

**PROVIDING REASSURANCES** Another part of a community's reaction to a new facility is based on the fear of change. It upsets community equilibrium and endangers familiar ways of doing things. Fears are usually exaggerated because they are based on fragmentary knowledge and rumors. Some of the techniques of squelching rumors must therefore be employed:

▶ Establish an information center (usually the public information office of the incoming organization).
▶ Be alert to misinformation about your organization.
▶ Conduct a community survey, if justified.
▶ Spike the rumor with accurate, reliable information to those groups where rumor exists.
▶ Assign one person as the spokesperson for the organization.
▶ Hold meetings with special groups, e.g.,
Local personnel managers who may be concerned about new pattern of wages and benefits.
Local school officals and teachers who may worry about influx of new students.

**GETTING ACQUAINTED** The community relations objective of opening a new plant or facility is to get to know your new neighbors and to let them get to know you. An organization has to initiate a lot of information exchange and, even more important, get involved in the community. The responsibilities of being a community citizen have to be accepted.

Some standard procedures for becoming better acquainted are:

▶ Identify your new neighbors. Get to know something about them.

▶ A door-to-door survey of close neighbors—and a sample of others in the community—is a good way to know what people think about you. Give special attention to community leaders. They are most concerned and influential.

▶ Introduce yourself to the local media.

▶ Hold a dedication ceremony that involves:
Meeting (and, in most cases, a luncheon) with community leaders.
Open house for general public.
Special event for new employees and their families. (Note: If necessary, schedule a separate day for each of these events.)

▶ Join local organizations.

▶ Create a community council that meets regularly.

| Preparing for a New Plant | Assigned to | Date/Time Assigned | Date/Time Completed |
|---|---|---|---|
| I. Check with the real property manager, the proposed new plant manager, and CEO as to where the plant will be located and all factual material as to location selection. | _____ | _____ | _____ |
| II. Determine the local public attitude through door-to-door interviews of area residents.<br>1. Notify local political leaders in advance.<br>2. Identify opinion leaders for the neighborhood as well as the town.<br>Include:<br>a. Traffic officer.<br>b. Highway users to school.<br>c. Other area road users.<br>d. Environmental group heads.<br>e. Beneficiaries (merchants, suppliers).<br>f. Police and fire department heads. | _____ | _____ | _____ |
| III. Visit pertinent news media—print and electronic—which cover the proposed area. | _____ | _____ | _____ |
| IV. Check with real property manager and appropriate town officers as to existing zoning bylaws and/or modifications.<br>1. If modifications in the bylaws are required, public hearings must be held.<br>2. If the above step is required, clearly state the company's position and commitment regarding the benefits to the town on CEO's signature. Notify local news media.<br>3. At public hearings, have CEO or designated spokesman make no commitments which cannot be kept. | _____ | _____ | _____ |
| V. When the above is completed, present architectural elevations together with physical data—such as employment and payroll figures—to the townspeople through the local media. | _____ | _____ | _____ |

*(continued)*

| Preparing for a New Plant | Assigned to | Date/Time Assigned | Date/Time Completed |
|---|---|---|---|
| 1. Pay special attention to potential violations of the visual and physical environment. Take steps to mitigate any controversial or provocative aspects. | | | |
| 2. Consider plantings, lowering of roof line, accommodating architectural style of the neighborhood. | | | |
| VI. Prepare a statement of total cost of construction, the amount to be spent with local contractors and suppliers, the number of people you will hire, and the impact on the income and tax base of the community. | _____ | _____ | _____ |
| 1. Include statements by the local economic development commission chairperson and his on her opposite number at state levels. | | | |
| VII. Arrange for the soil-breaking ceremony and the presence of VIP's and townspeople. In each case a senior member of management must be present. The press should be encouraged to use photos and TV cameras. Emphasize the contract for landscaping and planting. | _____ | _____ | _____ |
| VIII. Announce a date for plant opening and ceremonies. | _____ | _____ | _____ |

# 29

# PLANT OPENINGS, BUILDINGS, AND EXPANSIONS

A plant opening or expansion is a "natural" event—a kind of addition to the family. As such, announcements, an open house, and a celebration are not only appropriate but expected. It is a time for speeches about growth opportunities for employees, a broader job and tax base for the community, and renewed faith in the American economic system. It is also a publicity opportunity to gain greater awareness of the company and its products.

The checklist extends the broader considerations previously discussed in preparing for a new plant.

| Plant Openings, Buildings, and Expansions | Assigned to | Date/Time Assigned | Date/Time Completed |
|---|---|---|---|
| I.  Symbolize the opening of a plant by more than a ribbon cutting ceremony. Consider:<br>　1.  Establishing a town fountain in front of the building.<br>　2.  Naming a doorway, wing, or section after the founder of the town. | _____ | _____ | _____ |
| II.  Place ads in the local media to invite the community members to the opening. | _____ | _____ | _____ |
| III.  Plan a permanent tour of the entire premises.<br>　1.  Stanchions, ribbons, and signs are imperative. Signs should identify what work will take place in each area.<br>　2.  Provide more than enough guides—select competent people for this job.<br>　3.  Prepare a take-away brochure that includes:<br>　　a.  Short history of the company.<br>　　b.  CEO statement on commitment to community.<br>　　c.  Description of what will take place in the new plant.<br>　　d.  How many people will work there.<br>　　e.  Effect of tax rate.<br>　　f.  Sample of product, if feasible.<br>　4.  Have enough photographers on hand to capture appropriate pictures for use in local media and arrange for prints to be sent to those in photos. Try to include as many people in the photos as possible. | _____ | _____ | _____ |
| IV.  Invite:<br>　1.  Employees, prospective employees, and their families.<br>　2.  Labor officials, VIPs, leading customers (by telephone or personal note).<br>　3.  Stockholders in nearby communities.<br>　4.  Plant backers and neighbors. | _____ | _____ | _____ |

(continued)

| Plant Openings, Buildings, and Expansions | Assigned to | Date/Time Assigned | Date/Time Completed |
|---|---|---|---|
| V. Make company cafeteria available; provide refreshments. | _____ | _____ | _____ |
| VI. Lay out appropriate parking spaces that show ease of entrance and exit without interfering with local traffic. | _____ | _____ | _____ |
| VII. Station appropriate security guards inside and outside of plant. | _____ | _____ | _____ |
| VIII. Arrange for a welcoming committee which should include plant manager, other company officers, and CEO. | _____ | _____ | _____ |
| IX. Check insurance policy for liability for loss of guests' personal belongings. | _____ | _____ | _____ |

# 30

# PLANT CLOSINGS

A plant closing pits a company's economic rights of mobility against its social responsibilities to employees and the local community where it has done business. Not satisfied with business' recognition of its responsibility, some unions curtail these economic rights through contract clauses. Similarly, some state governments have passed or are considering legislation that spells out the obligations of a company that wishes to close or relocate a plant.

Some of these obligations are:

- ► Advance notification of plans to close a plant.
- ► Time periods range from sixty days to two years.
- ► Helping employees find other employment.
- ► Allowing early retirement.
- ► Providing severance pay.

A reasonable advance notice period must be decided upon. If it is too far in advance, a company's credit standing with local banks is impaired, customers who may worry about obtaining spare parts may be lost, and work morale and productivity will slip. If notice is given too late, workers and the community cannot plan adequately for this shock.

Every possible effort should be made to explore ways with local leaders and employees to keep a facility open. That is an advantage of early notification. In some cases, communities have made tax concessions, made loans, or found other ways of helping a company. Employees have accepted wage reductions or postponed wage increases. When violation of environmental requirements has been the reason for moving, the community has sometimes banded together to put pressure on the Environmental Protection Agency for an extension of deadlines or modification of standards.

If the facility cannot be kept open, some companies work with industrial development agencies to attract new industry. Funds are sometimes donated to such campaigns. In a few cases, the company has donated its land and industrial facilities to the local community.

When a decision to close is made, the company should fully explain its reasons. Employees and the community have a "right to know."

One caution: When a plant closing has a significant impact on the community, the announcement should be treated as a "material fact" in financial relations terms. No one individual or group should get advance notice of the closing. A public announcement must be made so everyone in the community is equally informed at the same time.

| **Plant Closings** | **Assigned to** | **Date/Time Assigned** | **Date/Time Completed** |
|---|---|---|---|
| I. Recognize that a plant closing is a traumatic experience to employees and community. | _____ | _____ | _____ |
| II. Don't abruptly shock affected persons. Instead:<br>1. Give hints of closing—tell of decline in demand for product, etc.<br>2. Publicize efforts of alternate projects to keep the plant open.<br>3. Publicize the possibility of selling the plant to someone else who would operate on the same level of employment and taxability. | _____ | _____ | _____ |
| III. Publicize the closing of the plant to:<br>1. Stockholders and financial media.<br>2. Employees.<br>3. Customers.<br>4. Community.<br>5. Suppliers.<br>6. Your industry. | _____ | _____ | _____ |
| IV. State in positive terms the pragmatics of the change, and how the slack will be picked up as far as employees and other publics are concerned. | _____ | _____ | _____ |
| V. Transfer as many employees as possible to equal-level jobs that are in the same general vicinity as the closing plant. | _____ | _____ | _____ |
| VI. Accommodate the shortened time to retirement for those who are near it. | _____ | _____ | _____ |
| VII. Seek other jobs in other organizations for those who cannot transfer or cannot be employed by the company. | _____ | _____ | _____ |
| VIII. Set up an employment office in plant, and provide professional assistance. | _____ | _____ | _____ |

*(continued)*

| Plant Closings | Assigned to | Date/Time Assigned | Date/Time Completed |
|---|---|---|---|
| IX. Recognize that a certain amount of attrition and unemployment will occur. | _____ | _____ | _____ |
| X. Send news release to community media summarizing the net effect of all the efforts to transfer, re-employ, or rehire former employees. | _____ | _____ | _____ |

# 31

# COMMUNITY LINES OF ORGANIZATION

An organization's lines of communication extend far beyond the traditional organization chart. One place they extend to is the local community. The line that legally separates an organization from the community is crossed daily by employees and other community members who affect or are affected by the organization. One of the key tasks of a community relations specialist, therefore, is to maintain a file of these "community members" of the organization.

**COMMUNITY MEMBER FILE** The focus of any community member file is its leaders. They are the ones whose decisions affect the welfare of the organization and who serve as communications intermediaries with other community members. The list begins with local government officials: the mayor, deputy mayor, city council members, heads of major departments. It includes the heads of major economic institutions, such as other company presidents, bank presidents, the head of the local chamber of commerce, etc. Also, not to be overlooked, are leaders of relevant voluntary organizations typically categorized as follows:

- ► Veterans, military, patriotic.
- ► Civic, service, or both.
- ► Lodges, fraternal, or professional.
- ► Cultural, educational, college, or alumni.
- ► Social, sports, hobby, or recreational.
- ► Church or religious.
- ► Political or pressure.

## LEADER IDENTIFICATION

Help in identifying leaders can be obtained from the local chamber of commerce, a predecessor, and cooperative newspaper editors and broadcasters. This method can be followed up with the sociometric approach of asking each community leader who he or she thinks other leaders might be. In addition, the local media should be scanned for reference to other leaders.

## COMMUNICATION LINKS

This list of community leaders and the groups they represent is an invaluable reference for several kinds of communication links with the community:

- ► "Getting- acquainted" meetings to let community leaders know about your organization and to learn first hand what the needs of the community are.
- ► Joining key social and civic groups for the purpose of getting involved in community activities in keeping in touch with community public opinion.
- ► Forming company community councils for an exchange of information and views and a way of solving mutual problems.

| **Community Lines of Communication** | **Assigned to** | **Date/Time Assigned** | **Date/Time Completed** |
|---|---|---|---|
| I. Build a reliable cadre of community influentials. | _____ | _____ | _____ |

I.  Build a reliable cadre of community influentials.

   1.  Survey each HQ plant and facility community for those individuals who make area opinion decisions, such as these obvious ones:

      a.  Publishers of daily and weekly newspapers, and special purpose publications.

      b.  Owners and managers of TV and radio stations.

      c.  Police and fire chiefs.

      d.  Bank presidents and directors.

      e.  CEOs of largest employers.

      f.  Principal municipal officers.

   2.  List also those not so obvious persons whose weight is also significant:

      a.  Leading attorneys.

      b.  Leading realtors.

      c.  Leading insurance agency owners.

      d.  Utility company managers.

      e.  Postmaster.

      f.  School superintendent and principals.

      g.  Heads of service clubs or groups.

      h.  Executive secretaries of chambers of commerce or board of trade.

      i.  Leaders of municipal political committees.

      j.  Head of PTA.

      k.  Owners/managers of major retail establishments.

      l.  Owners of principal automobile dealerships.

      m. Largest property taxpayer.

      n.  Head of youth group.

      o.  Head of central labor committee.

*(continued)*

| Community Lines of Communication | Assigned to | Date/Time Assigned | Date/Time Completed |
|---|---|---|---|
| II. Have your CEO invite a number of persons from this list and establish an ad hoc group which will have regular monthly or bi-monthly luncheon meetings.<br>   1. Choose a name for the group, something not self-serving:<br>     a. "Townies."<br>     b. "In-Towners."<br>     c. "Community Club."<br>     d. "Long-Range Planners."<br>     e. Any address would do as title.<br>   2. Have an agenda for each meeting, which impinges directly or indirectly on your problems and ones common to your organization and others in the area.<br>     a. Also discuss plans and implement plans of benefit to the general populace.<br>     b. Use the group as the problem-solving panel. | _____ | _____ | _____ |
| III. Arrange for DPR to phone or visit members of the panel on a frequent, but not annoying, basis. | _____ | _____ | _____ |
| IV. Have the group sponsor scholarships generally oriented to your problem.<br>   1. Arrange for visits from celebrities in the field of interest to attend your group luncheons.<br>   2. Erect a monument to some local hero or teacher.<br>   3. Set annual summer and winter bashes for area kids.<br>   4. Arrange to have taken a motion picture for local TV viewing of the community and its highlights. | _____ | _____ | _____ |

*(continued)*

| **Community Lines of Communication** | Assigned to | Date/Time Assigned | Date/Time Completed |
|---|---|---|---|
| V. Maintain constant contact and control of the group and use the meetings not only as a consumer or attitude panel, but as a sounding board for projects and problems. On infrequent occasions you can use a telephone network to the members to effect a ground swell of sentiment for your needs and/or those of others in area. | _____ | _____ | _____ |

# VII

# FINANCIAL RELATIONS

Raising capital to start a business and manage its continued growth is a central concern of all managers. Relations with stockholders and others in the financial community are accorded high priority by the CEO. Not only the company's, but the CEO's own welfare depends on the financial community's appraisal of his or her performance.

**VALUE OF HIGH P/E RATIO** Performance in financial relations is measured by the market price commanded by a company's stocks. A more precise measure is the price/earnings ratio. It is calculated by dividing the market price by the earnings per share. The p/e ratio would be compared with that of other companies in a given industry with stocks, in general. Glamour stocks have sold at p/e ratios in excess of 50.

A high p/e ratio keeps stockholders content. They are more likely to hold on to the company's stocks and not sell out when a tender offer is made by another company or opposition group that wants to win management control. This loyalty helps the CEO to keep his or her job.

Loyal stockholders also become a prime source of additional capital when the company decides to issue new stock. When a company seeks acquisitions by offering its stocks in exchange, a high p/e ratio is also of obvious advantage.

**KEY PUBLICS** Stockholders are the prime target of financial relations. Nationwide there were just under 30 million individual investors in 1980 and they are getting younger all the time. According to a New York Stock Exchange survey, these investors have a median age of 45½, compared with 52½ five years ago. Of all new adult shareholders, 48 percent are under 35 years old. The portfolio holdings of the typical adult shareholder is valued at $4,000. Male shareholders outnumber female ones by about 500,000, but of new shareholders, 55 percent are women.

Individual stockholders account for a shrinking share of trading volume. Institutions account for more than 70 percent of it. These institutions comprise

- ► Pension funds.
- ► Investment companies; e.g., mutual funds.
- ► College and university endowments.
- ► Foundations.
- ► Bank trust departments.
- ► Insurance companies.
- ► Profit-sharing funds.
- ► Investment clubs and groups.

Well-informed and trained professionals make investment decisions for these institutional investors. Compared with individual investors, they require more back-up materials. The same is true of other important financial relations publics:

- ► Security analysts.
- ► Investment counselors.
- ► Brokerage houses.
- ► Investment banks.
- ► Financial press.
- ► Statistical services.

Security analysts deserve special mention. They are employed by all of the institutions that buy and sell stocks or give stock-market advice.

Their function is to evaluate and interpret on a continuous basis the financial affairs of companies. They judge the worth of corporate securities under a variety of situations and circumstances. Hence they are a key target audience of financial communications.

**SEC REQUIREMENTS** Full and timely disclosure of information is the paramount requirement of financial relations. Every investor, including anybody who wants to become an investor, must be given enough timely information to enable him or her to make an intelligent buying and selling decision. This requirement is set forth by the Securities and Exchange Commission (SEC) which polices the securities markets.

After the disastrous stock-market crash of October 1929, faith in an uncontrolled market collapsed. One of the cornerstones of New Deal legislation was the passage of new securities regulations:

► The Securities Act of 1933 requires a full disclosure of all material facts regarding the issuance of new securities before they are offered for sale. The purpose is to enable an investor to make an intelligent judgment of a security before it is bought.

► The Securities Exchange Act of 1934 has three purposes: (1) to eliminate fraud, manipulation, and other abuses in the trading of securities both on the organized exchanges and in the over-the-counter markets; (2) to make available to the public, information regarding the condition of corporations whose securities are listed on any national securities exchange; and (3) to regulate the use of the nation's credit in securities trading.

In administering these laws, the SEC emphasizes two words: "full" and "timely" disclosure. Full disclosure means that any "material fact" that could affect stock values must be disseminated. It is always easy to look back and determine what information affected stock prices. Such reviews indicate that activities such as these are likely to have an impact:

► Dividends—especially a change from past announcements.
► Earnings reports—annual and quarterly.
► Mergers and acquisitions.
► Major product developments and discoveries.

► Expansion plans.
► Stock splits.
► Key management changes.
► Contracts and awards.

Timely disclosure means that everyone who wants to engage in stock-market activities has equal access to material facts at the same time others do. No one can take advantage of prior knowledge or early information to buy or sell before the market reacts to the disclosed information.

That SEC ideal is, of course, never reached because some investors make it their business to stay closer to financial news sources than the average investor does. Someone sitting in a broker's office hears about something before others read about it in the evening paper or next morning's paper. Furthermore, an experienced or professional investor has the background and knowledge with which to interpret information.

Recognizing these limitations, the SEC simply tries to come as close as possible to its ideal model. One way it does this is to require immediate and simultaneous disclosure of information of such significant events as a dividend decision. Using the speediest means of delivery, a company must inform Dow Jones & Company, Inc. (the key financial newswire service) and one or more other major national newswire services, such as Reuter Economic Services, the Associated Press (AP), or United Press International (UPI). Major newspapers should also be informed. If the news is apt to result in drastic change in the stock price, the company must also notify the stock exchange where its stocks are listed: the Telephone Alert of the Department of Stock List of the New York Stock Exchange (NYSE) or the Securities Division of the American Stock Exchange (AMEX).

Another way the SEC tries to give everyone equal access to information is to forbid "insider trading." Officers and anyone else employed by a corporation—including public relations practitioners—who come into the possession of information in the course of their business activities are prohibited from market dealings until all investors have had an opportunity to receive the same information. "Tipees" who receive such information from insiders or third parties face the same restriction. AMEX suggests a waiting period of at least twenty-four hours.

Accuracy—important in all communications—becomes a sanctified standard in financial relations. The SEC has been pressing hard to make all professional groups involved with financial information—auditors, underwriters, lawyers, and public relations practitioners—assume more responsibility. In the well-publicized "Pig 'n Whistle" case, a public relations firm was charged with issuing press releases and other materials that "contained false and misleading statements and omitted to state material facts."

The Financial Code of Ethics of the Public Relations Society of America (PRSA) is aimed at correcting such situations. It requires that PRSA members engaged in financial public relations know the securities laws, doublecheck such material facts as earning projections, encourage clients to disclose significant information, and actively attempt to correct false or misleading information circulating about a client's business.

**ORGANIZING FOR FINANCIAL RELATIONS**

Financial relations constitutes more than meeting legal requirements. The corporate secretary, treasurer, and legal counsel concentrate on the legalities of preparing official filings and annual reports, sending out proxy statements, holding annual meetings, and supervising the transfer agent and registrar. Public relations practitioners look at the opportunities inherent in these contacts to strengthen the understanding stockholders and members of the financial community have of the company and to build positive attitudes.

About half of the large corporations have specialized investor relations departments that can concentrate on achieving a fair p/e ratio, building the loyalty of stockholders, and gaining a high valuation of company performance. The heads of investor relations departments are often vice presidents and report either to a chief financial officer (CFO) or directly to the CEO. Where a separate IR department does not exist, the public relations staff handles financial relations in close cooperation with the CFO. Where investor relations is a major part of public relations, the department is sometimes called "Investor and Public Relations."

The basic ingredients of a sound stockholder relations program are:

> ► Letter of welcome to new stockholders, signed by the CEO.
> ► Corporate fact book.
> ► Annual report.
> ► Interim reports.
> ► Annual meeting.
> ► Post-meeting report.

In addition, the total financial relations program would include:

- ► Financial publicity.
- ► Security analyst meetings.
- ► Financial advertising.

Financial publicity satisfies the needs of the business and financial editors and professionals in financial institutions. Through these media and services the stockholders are also kept better informed about company affairs in the times between interim and annual reports.

Financial advertising is sometimes useful as a supplement to the total financial relations program. Some companies hope that these messages might reach potential investors who might not otherwise hear about the company. Also, the attention of financial opinion leaders might be attracted so as to motivate them to send for additional information.

Another activity of financial relations is a stockholder survey—and, sometimes, a survey of security analysts. Before undertaking such an optional activity, the practitioner should first analyze internal information:

- ► Number of stockholders.
- ► Geographical distribution of stockholders.
- ► Concentration of ownership of stocks.
- ► Turnover rate.
- ► Percentage of proxies returned.
- ► Analysis of proxy votes for and against management.

# 32

# ANNUAL MEETINGS

Most companies are legally required to hold an annual meeting of their stockholders. State articles of incorporation and individual company by-laws make this requirement. The Securities and Exchange Commission and stock exchanges imply such a requirement and certainly encourage the holding of annual meetings.

Some chief executive officers endure this legal requirement. As stated by Bill Abrams of *The Wall Street Journal:*

> To many corporate chairmen, annual meetings are about as welcome as surprise visits from Internal Revenue Service auditors. More than one chief executive has been known to joke that he'd do just about anything to avoid his yearly grilling by shareholders.

One of the CEOs who expressed this disdain for annual meetings is J. B. Fuqua of Fuqua Industries, Inc. He says that "the continued practice of having an annual ritual which we represent to be a meeting of the stockholders, is a farce, if it is not, indeed, a fraud."

Most CEOs, however, see the annual meeting as a symbol of corporate democracy and the operation of the free enterprise system. The occasion allows a report of their stewardship of the companies they head. It is one of the only places available for the CEO to get feedback about how he or she is performing on the job.

Equally important, the annual meeting is a special event that can serve as a publicity platform for media attention. Almost all publicity-held companies invite the news media. It is not only *The Wall Street Journal* and *The New York Times* that provide coverage; regional and local newspapers give increasing attention to annual meetings in their business and financial pages—so do magazines and specialized newsletters. The preparation and distribution of news releases, holding news conferences, and providing individual interviews with company officers are routine activities.

If the meeting is held at company headquarters, some companies use the occasion to support their community relations and employee relations efforts. When stockholders are seen as potential customers, marketing efforts such as displays, product demonstrations, and handouts are planned for annual meetings.

Instead of seeing the annual meeting as a legal ritual, the opportunities inherent in this special event should be seized.

CEOs and other top managers must be prepared, however, to face some tough questions. Some come from "professional" stockholders who make it their business to attend selected meetings and prod management. Best known are Lewis D. and John J. Gilbert, who represent the interests of small stockholders and like to raise question about:

- ► "Excessive" executive compensation, pension plans, and stock options.
- ► Scheduling of meetings in out-of-the-way places.
- ► Good ratio of outside to inside directors.
- ► Cumulative voting (which they consider a "right" of small stockholders).
- ► Stagger-system of voting for board members whereby only one out of two or more "classes" of board members is elected each year (making it more difficult for an opposition to win board seats).

Another well-known independent stockholder is Wilma Soss, President of the Federation of Women Stockholders. Espousing the cause of electing more women to boards of directors, she has often been physically removed from meetings by security guards after being ruled out of order and causing disruption.

Since the late '60s and early '70s, social activists have appeared at annual meetings, mainly to raise questions about a company's social performance. An activist simply has to buy one share of a company's stock to gain admittance. As a stockholder, he or she is also allowed to submit proposals to management for inclusion in the company's proxy form and proxy materials sent to all stockholders of a specified record date. The SEC acts as a referee in disputes over whether certain proposals are proper to the business of the annual meeting. Its interpretation has been generous to social action groups. Such issues as doing business in South Africa, manufacturing certain military products, establishing a social responsibility committee on the board of directors, and the hiring of women and minority workers have been considered appropriate by the SEC.

| Annual Meetings | Assigned to | Date/Time Assigned | Date/Time Completed |
|---|---|---|---|
| I. Besides fulfilling a legal requirement and taking care of normal business such as election of directors, auditing firm, etc., consider the following opportunities in your annual meeting:<br>  1. Demonstrating new products.<br>  2  Distributing samples and appropriate sales literature.<br>  3. Holding a forum on public issues of concern to the company. | _____ | _____ | _____ |
| II. Hold the annual meeting in the city where the principal office of the corporation is located or select a place convenient to stockholders by:<br>  1. Holding meeting in any accessible large city in the country.<br>  2. Holding meeting where there is a concentration of stockholders.<br>  3. Rotating place of meeting to different regions of the country.<br>  4. Arranging for closed circuit telecasting of annual meeting in large cities where stockholders are concentrated. | _____ | _____ | _____ |
| III. Prepare an encompassing agenda.<br>  1. Prepare a list of questions that vocal stockholders, activist stockholders, news media and visitors (if allowed) are likely to raise.<br>    a. Develop a list of possible questions by examining:<br>      ► Publications of the American Society of Corporate Secretaries, Inc. (9 Rockefeller Plaza, New York, NY 10020).<br>      ► Transcripts or reports of previous annual meetings.<br>      ► Correspondence with stockholders during the year.<br>      ► Observation of discussion areas at other companies' annual meetings. | _____ | _____ | _____ |

(continued)

| | Annual Meetings | Assigned to | Date/Time Assigned | Date/Time Completed |
|---|---|---|---|---|
| | ► Names of stockholders planning to attend the meeting who are known to ask certain kinds of questions. | | | |
| b. | Familiarize yourself with shareholder proxy resolutions prepared by such organizations as: | | | |
| | ► Interfaith Center on Corporate Responsibility, 475 Riverside Drive, Room 566, New York, NY 10027. It focuses on these issues: agribusiness, bank voting of stocks, community reinvestment, domestic equality, energy, infant formula, militarism, transnational corporations, and human development. | | | |
| | ► Investor Responsibility Research Center, Inc. 1522 K Street, N.W., Suite 730, Washington DC 20005. IRRC provides four types of research services for its subscribers: Proxy Issues Reports, Special Issues Reports, South Africa Review Service Reports, and a monthly newsletter (*News for Investors*) that informs investors of pending shareholder resolutions. | | | |
| 2. | Prepare a "blue book" containing answers to probable questions to be asked. | | | |
| a. | Include data such as book value per share, advertising expenditures, amounts of charitable contributions, and other questions likely to be asked. | | | |
| b. | Go through a dry run of questions and answers, and determine which officer is best equipped to handle each question. | | | |

*(continued)*

| **Annual Meetings** | Assigned to | Date/Time Assigned | Date/Time Completed |
|---|---|---|---|
| 3. Hold direct discussions with spokespersons of responsible activist groups.<br>  a. Review meeting procedures to ensure that all stockholders will be able to express their views.<br>  b. If proposals have been submitted for inclusion in proxy statement, consider resolving the issues through a process of accommodation. | | | |
| IV. Prepare physical and mechanical accommodations for the meeting:<br>1. See Sales Meetings and Conventions checklist.<br>2. Arrange for voter and proxy check-in desk.<br>3. Arrange for responsible enumerators.<br>  a. Give totals to chairman or corporate secretary just as meeting begins.<br>  b. Make allowance to add voters/proxies of latecomers. | _____ | _____ | _____ |
| V. Plan security and admissions policy for annual meeting:<br>1. Use an advance registration system by requesting in the proxy materials that stockholders write for meeting admission tickets.<br>2. Refer those without admission tickets to an area separate and apart from the entrance where necessary admission procedures can be followed. (Any resulting disturbance would thereby be isolated stockholders' entry to meeting hall.)<br>3. Provide for free checking service for those attending and, if deemed necessary, require the inspection of all valises, briefcases, packages, etc., before being checked or brought into the meeting room. | _____ | _____ | _____ |

*(continued)*

| **Annual Meetings** | **Assigned to** | **Date/Time Assigned** | **Date/Time Completed** |
|---|---|---|---|
| 4. Do not permit signs, bullhorns, flash attachments for cameras, and tape recorders to be brought into the meeting room. | | | |
| 5. Instruct security personnel on procedures to be followed in the event of a disturbance. | | | |
| VI. Use ground rules so that meeting will be conducted in fairness and good faith. | _____ | _____ | _____ |
| 1. Chairman should state at the beginning of the meeting that he or she plans to follow order of business as set forth in the agenda. | | | |
| a. Distribute agenda prior to start of meeting. | | | |
| 2. In place of *Robert's Rules of Order*—which may be too formal for the annual meeting—announce the ground rules that will be used. For example: | | | |
| a. Ask stockholders who wish to be recognized by the Chair during the discussion period to stand or raise their hands and give their names. | | | |
| b. Announce that a microphone will be made available, or state where the microphones are placed. | | | |
| c. Have an adequate number of microphones for stockholders. (They resent seeing officers with individual microphones while they have only one.) | | | |
| d. Avoid asking stockholders to write their questions on distributed cards. | | | |
| e. Suggest that comments be kept as brief as possible and, if necessary, impose a time limit, e.g., two minutes for each comment. | | | |
| 3. Recognize stockholder queries, including those of vocal stockholders and activists; do not try to brush them aside. | | | |

*(continued)*

| Annual Meetings | Assigned to | Date/Time Assigned | Date/Time Completed |
|---|---|---|---|
| 4. Be courteous, not patronizing. | | | |
| 5. Answer each question fully and directly. | | | |
|   a. The American Society of Corporate Secretaries, Inc. reports: "Experience indicates that a Chairman who refuses to answer without given a reason, or who shows resentment over a question or comment, may well find it difficult to maintain control over the meeting" (Guide for the Conduct of Annual Meetings, 1970). | | | |
| VII. Follow the agenda. | _____ | _____ | _____ |
| 1. Do not allow film and slide presentations to encroach on the time shareholders are allowed to air their views. | | | |
|   a. Cut back on long speeches if visual material is shown. | | | |
|   b. Consider showing films before the meeting begins or after the question and answer period. | | | |
| VIII. Prepare a contingency plan for the event of potential disruption of the meeting. Adopt an emergency procedure to effect promptly the election of directors and other required legal action so that the meeting can be quickly adjourned. | _____ | _____ | _____ |
| IX. After the meeting, prepare and issue: | _____ | _____ | _____ |
| 1. Minutes of stockholders' meeting. | | | |
| 2. Post-meeting report to stockholders. | | | |
| X. Have the Chairman announce at least one significant item of news value: | _____ | _____ | _____ |
| 1. Financial results. | | | |
| 2. Predictions. | | | |
| 3. Scientific. | | | |
| 4. Product. | | | |
| 5. Acquisition or merger. | | | |

# 33

# ANNUAL AND INTERIM REPORTS

Besides being a legal requirement, the annual report is the key source of information about a company for small, individual stockholders. It is also a basic document used by security analysts, researchers, and other professionals in the financial community.

Emphasis is on financial data. The balance sheet lists a company's assets, liabilities, and stockholder equity. It is a snapshot of the financial worth of the company. The other key financial statement is the profit and loss (or income) statement which shows the sources of revenue, the expenses of doing business, and the resulting profit (or loss) for the past fiscal year. The previous year's and quarter's results are added for comparison.

Technical jargon should be avoided in these financial statements to enable the average investor to determine what is actually happening in the company. The place for accounting language is in the 10-K form required by the SEC and which is made available to any stockholder. The report should state the essential facts about the company's activities and its financial status in clear, simple terms.

When a company does not publish a separate "fact book," the annual report can serve the purpose of describing its business more fully than is done in the typical, terse statement on the inside cover. An unusual example is Kimberly-Clark Corporation's 1977 Annual Report which contained over fifty pages of information: the corporate profile, product classes, selected market information, senior executive management, corporate organizational structure, description of operating units, etc.

In its design, style, and content, the annual report is a major representation of the company's identity—its character, management style, and outlook. The report must portray the company in a distinctive manner. Its unique strengths and personality should be reflected throughout the report. Photographs showing plant locations, industrial processes, employees at work, and other colorful scenes help to project a feeling of the company.

The chairperson's and/or president's letter to the stockholders is an excellent vehicle for the top officer to reflect his or her vision of the company and its future. It is also an opportunity to portray his or her own personality and to avoid the look-alike nature of most of these letters. On the other hand, the report should not become an ego-boost device at the expense of representing the company as a whole.

Increasingly, the annual report includes information about a company's social performance, hiring of minority employees, philanthropic contributions, environmental protection, etc. However, some companies are now issuing separate social reports because of the voluminous number of activities to cover and the high interest by audiences other than stockholders.

For companies greatly affected by the socio-political environment (and most are), another subject area of annual reports is a statement of public issues affecting the company. Companies realize that many of their stockholders are opinion leaders or active citizens who may be motivated to become political allies.

Consumer product companies find a marketing opportunity in annual reports. Auto manufacturers typically show their new models. Especially when a company follows the policy of broadening their base of stock ownership and therefore has numerous stockholders, such consumer-oriented material has great marketing value. The Quaker Oats Annual Report 1980 has a front cover showing its well-positioned product mix of Corn Bran, Quaker Oats, and Aunt Jemima Lite. Its contents include five full pages of color photographs of major product innovations and illustrations of their diversified products.

Next to the annual report, interim (usually quarterly) reports are most important forms of communication with stockholders. They keep stockholders informed of changes in the financial status of the company. Thereby the frequent criticism by stockholders that they first hear about important developments in the newspapers before their company informs them is overcome. Interim reports can be used for a wide variety of purposes. Some companies follow the practice of incorporating their annual meeting report into the first-quarter interim report. When companies are interested in stockholders as a political constituency, the interim report becomes a major vehicle for strong stockholder relations.

| **Annual And Interim Reports** | **Assigned to** | **Date/Time Assigned** | **Date/Time Completed** |
|---|---|---|---|
| I.   1. If your organization does not employ a consultant for this purpose, obtain and read the SEC regulations concerning: | _____ | _____ | _____ |

I.   1. If your organization does not employ a consultant for this purpose, obtain and read the SEC regulations concerning:
- a. Writing requirements.
- b. Prohibitions.
- c. Prospectuses.
- d. Proxies.
- e. Full disclosure.
- f. Advertising.
- g. 10-K's and their relationship to annual reports.
- h. CEO's predictions.
- i. Financial material (auditor).

2. Copies of SEC regulations can be obtained by writing to: Div. of Corp., Finance, Securities & Exchange Comm., 500 N. Capital St., Washington DC 20549.

3. In addition to obligatory financial and other reports to be supplied by outside auditors, determine the design and content of the report for:
- a. Cover.
- b. Photography.
- c. Illustrative charts, etc.
- d. Chairperson's/President's letter.
- e. "Boiler plate" or body copy.

4. Make it readable:
- a. Use plain language. Write, "Our products are selling well," instead of "Our established products continue to exhibit strong consumer acceptance."
- b. Be candid; e.g., "We had a very bad year in 1981."

*(continued)*

| **Annual And Interim Reports** | **Assigned to** | **Date/Time Assigned** | **Date/Time Completed** |
|---|---|---|---|
| c. Write in layers: present the information to several different levels of readership—from the most casual skimmer to the serious security analyst. | | | |
| d. Try not to be fuzzy, abstract, stuffy, or stodgy. | | | |
| 5. Consider printing annual report in foreign languages if overseas operations are important. | | | |
| 6. Consider whether there should be a consistent program of making all photography oriented to: | | | |
| a. Products. | | | |
| b. Procedures. | | | |
| c. Plants and facilities. | | | |
| d. Personnel. | | | |
| 7. Obtain a file of other companies' annual reports of different types and styles. | | | |
| a. Study these for suggestions and ideas to determine your own specific type of report. | | | |
| b. Decide whether your report should be a top quality, glossy paper, corporate sales tool, or, at the other extreme, an adequate meeting of the regulations. | | | |
| c. Get your printer to give you comparative price estimates before deciding which is best for your company. | | | |
| 8. Decide whether the president, or chairperson, or both will sign the letter. | | | |
| a. Decide who will actually write the letter. | | | |
| b. Get list of those who must approve the letter. | | | |

*(continued)*

| **Annual And Interim Reports** | **Assigned to** | **Date/Time Assigned** | **Date/Time Completed** |
|---|---|---|---|
| c. Determine how detailed CEO forecast will be. | | | |
| d. Determine whether it will be factual or have "sell." | | | |
| e. Select material for charts/graphs. | | | |
| f. Keep writing simple, direct, and understandable. | | | |
| g. Include company growth: ► Internally. ► Industrially. ► Research. ► Market share. ► Employee numbers. ► Physical properties. | | | |
| 9. Consider using separate, different colored section, perforated for easy pull-out of financial section for analysts, brokerage houses, etc. | | | |
| 10. Check to see that your auditing firm is one that is recognized and respected. | | | |
| 11. Determine the best method of report distribution: a. Fully enclosed first class. b. Unwrapped, but with stick label. c. Enclosed prospectus and proxy. d. Send to full financial list and pertinent influentials. | | | |
| 12. Be certain to give proper credit to all officers of parent and subsidiary companies as well as to directors. | | | |
| II. Consider making the interim reports selling tools by giving them serial quality, the cover in different colors for each quarter, and having a CEO letter interpret the required financial material. | _____ | _____ | _____ |

*(continued)*

| Annual And Interim Reports | Assigned to | Date/Time Assigned | Date/Time Completed |
|---|---|---|---|
| 1. Take advantage of pie charts for expenditures and costs vs. income. | | | |
| III. Determine the quantity of annual and interim reports kept on hand for distribution via inquiry, and for inclusion with pertinent news releases. | _____ | _____ | _____ |
| IV. Be certain that you follow the required standard forms and format. | _____ | _____ | _____ |
| V. Consider advantages vs. disadvantages of including the 10-K with your report rather than offering it to those interested enough to ask. | _____ | _____ | _____ |
| VI. Remember when in writing predictions and projections of earnings, sales, capital expenditures and future capital structure, plans and objectives, that SEC's "Safe Harbor" rules protects your company if all statements are made in good faith and on a reasonable basis for assumption. | _____ | _____ | _____ |
| VII. Be certain that your advertising manager and agency know every single restriction and prohibition in connection with financial advertising and promotional material of your company. Check out any deviation from standards with appropriate SEC official. | _____ | _____ | _____ |
| VIII. Remember that annual reports must be distributed to shareholders at least fifteen days before the annual meetings. Work back from the chosen dates to establish your work calendar for the report. | _____ | _____ | _____ |
|   1. Meet with division heads as well as CEO and financial and legal officers. | | | |
|   2. Give them work schedule for the report. | | | |
|   3. Develop and design the theme. | | | |
|   4. Set up the "dummy" layout. | | | |

*(continued)*

| Annual And Interim Reports | Assigned to | Date/Time Assigned | Date/Time Completed |
|---|---|---|---|
| 5. Get photographs, art work, charts, and graphs.<br>   a. Get the best photography possible, using action and color.<br>   b. Show executives and employees in work situations. | | | |
| 6. Check with printer for typography and art requirements. | | | |
| 7. Draft "boiler plate." | | | |
| 8. Draft President's/Chairperson's letter. | | | |
| 9. Get financial material from financial officer. | | | |
| 10. Get final material from auditors. | | | |
| 11. Clear final photographs and art work. | | | |
| 12. Clear final "boiler plate" and President's/Chairperson's letter. | | | |
| 13. Decide on printing and binding. | | | |
| 14. Arrange for mailing direct, through transfer agents, mailing house, or by other means. | | | |

# 34

# ACQUISITIONS AND MERGERS

Times are ripe for more acquisitions and mergers. The view that "big is bad" is losing ground in the face of harsh economic realities: global competition, stagnating productivity, and slow growth with high inflation. But not everyone agrees with this public policy position.

One consideration in deciding on and publicizing acquisitions and mergers is to justify them thoroughly from a public interest as well as company perspective. Antitrust laws and public opinion always loom in the background.

Because company growth is a material fact in an investment decision, dissemination of information to stockholders and the financial community is of paramount importance. And because it is a positive development, a company is motivated to publicize this news widely. A final consideration is that employees, local communities, and others who are affected deserve an explanation. Particular emphasis should be placed on what the impact will be and how the company will handle transition problems.

| Acquisitions and Mergers | Assigned to | Date/Time Assigned | Date/Time Completed |
|---|---|---|---|
| I. Meet with CEO and chairperson of Acquisition and Merger negotiation team.<br>  1. Determine full details of financial aspects of proposed arrangement.<br>  2. Determine effect on your own company's:<br>    a. Stock and shareholders.<br>    b. Employees.<br>    c. Plant facilities.<br>    d. Product line.<br>    e. Distribution network.<br>    f. Communities. | _____ | _____ | _____ |
| II. Check date of proposed merger and date of news release for conflicts and reactions. | _____ | _____ | _____ |
| III. Compile media release list:<br>  1. Stockholders.<br>  2. Financial.<br>  3. Employees.<br>  4. Communities.<br>  5. Industry press.<br>  6. Customers.<br>  7. Vendors.<br>  8. General public. | _____ | _____ | _____ |
| IV. Obtain approval of release from SEC. | _____ | _____ | _____ |
| V. Check with Department of Justice on possible antitrust action news. | _____ | _____ | _____ |
| VI. Send out news releases before and after votes by shareholders of both companies. | _____ | _____ | _____ |
| VII. Plan for major press conference at acquired company's headquarters. (See News Conferences Checklist.) | _____ | _____ | _____ |

(continued)

| Acquisitions and Mergers | Assigned to | Date/Time Assigned | Date/Time Completed |
|---|---|---|---|
| VIII. Plan for news coverage of your CEO's (designee) visit to each facility community of acquired company.<br>  1. Check out with local politicians and community leaders for possible "echoes" and/or assistance. | _____ | _____ | _____ |
| IX. Get feedback or report from your industrial relations manager's meetings with new division's union leaders. | _____ | _____ | _____ |
| X. Working with your advertising manager, determine how acquired company will be referred to in ads, etc.<br>  1. Be certain that acquired company's advertising, public relations, and promotion material is consistent with the parent company's policy.<br>  2. Meet with acquired company's DPR and PR consulting firm, as well as with the ad manager and agency. | _____ | _____ | _____ |
| XI. Ascertain new marketing plans of acquired company and write a release for trade papers and financial pages. | _____ | _____ | _____ |
| XII. Prepare and get approvals of letters from CEO outlining parent company's policies, predictions, and plans and send them to:<br>  1. Employees (enclosing company's employee handbook).<br>  2. Shareholders (enclosing latest annual and interim reports). | _____ | _____ | _____ |
| XIII. In the event of lay-offs of acquired company's employees because of redundancies, establish an employment office to assist in finding new jobs after all have been offered other jobs in other places of the parent company. | _____ | _____ | _____ |

*(continued)*

| Acquisitions and Mergers | Assigned to | Date/Time Assigned | Date/Time Completed |
|---|---|---|---|
| XIV. In the event of a shut-down of a facility of the acquired company, a senior officer must visit the town leaders before word of the shut-down is circulated. Soften the blow for local politicians and give them a chance to get other company occupancy. | _____ | _____ | _____ |
| XV. Announce progress of assimilation of acquired company in next interim report. Also send progress milestone news to financial and trade journals. | _____ | _____ | _____ |
| XVI. If your own company is acquired or merged into another organization, use the same checklist but assume the "flip" side. | _____ | _____ | _____ |

    1. Assure your executives and other employees of an honest assessment of their futures within the new company.

    2. Make every effort to eliminate from your employees' attitudes, an inimical or adversary relationship.

    3. Working with new DPR, communicate to all your company's employees, the facts of the merger, and point out the beneficial aspects to them.

    4. Letters should be written to all customers, dealers, and other external associations, the effect of the merger on them. Show them how they will benefit and explain the facts of the arrangements.

# 35

# FINANCING CHANGES

Reindustrialization has become a national priority. To improve productivity and raise profits, companies must find ways of financing needed changes.

Stockholders and financial institutions are the chief sources of capital. They must be convinced of the need for capital funds and the benefits that will accrue from investment. Changes in the tax structure are also of help in allowing companies to reinvest a greater protion of their earnings. Of special value are decreases in the corporate income tax, increases in depreciation allowances, and investment credits.

| Financing Changes | Assigned to | Date/Time Assigned | Date/Time Completed |
|---|---|---|---|
| I.   Meet with your organization's financial officer and legal counsel to obtain *every* fact:<br>1. Reason and need.<br>2. Importance and significance of change.<br>3. Timing.<br>4. Ramifications of:<br>   a. Company's position in industry.<br>   b. Stockholders and investors.<br>   c. Employees/union leaders.<br>   d. Communities.<br>   e. Government.<br>   f. Investment houses, security analysts, and investment counselors.<br>   g. Environmental and special interest groups. | _____ | _____ | _____ |
| II.  Check with appropriate government agencies (e.g., SEC and FTC) relative to requirements and prohibitions. | _____ | _____ | _____ |
| III. Draft a story as a result of the above and submit it to the CEO and the legal counsel for criticism and possible quotations and attribution. | _____ | _____ | _____ |
| IV.  Check out draft with pertinent government agency. | _____ | _____ | _____ |
| V.   Rewrite and resubmit draft to the CEO and attributor. | _____ | _____ | _____ |
| VI.  Release to:<br>1. Financial media.<br>2. Company employee publication.<br>3. Trade publications.<br>4. Community publications.<br>5. All company executives. | _____ | _____ | _____ |

# 36

# FIGHTING TAKEOVERS

Attempts by individuals, groups, or companies to gain control over a pub-
licly-held corporation are the subject of almost daily stories in business
and financial sections of newspapers. Some are friendly takeovers that
are welcomed by a company's management and shareholders. The one
more likely to make news and cause headaches for management are *raids*
by dissident shareholders and outsiders.

**PROXY FIGHTS AND**  Raids by insurgents take two forms: the proxy fight and the tender offer.
**TENDER OFFERS**  The proxy fight centers on whether incumbent management or the insurgent group is able to muster enough votes to elect its slate to the board
of directors. Each side tries to persuade shareholders to sign proxies
which gives it the right to vote the stock at the shareholders' meeting.

     Proxy fights follow the model of a political campaign of a two-party
system. The difference is that voters are shareholders and that the number of votes possessed by each is equal to the number of shares held.

Proxy solicitation firms help management in designing and executing a campaign to attract as many proxies as possible. Direct mail, telephone calls, regional meetings with shareholders, and many other techniques borrowed from political campaigns are used.

Tender offers are replacing proxy fights as the favorite instrument for gaining control. The insurgent simply makes an offer to buy a target company's shares directly from shareholders at a price that is well above the going market. This approach has several advantages:

1. Stocks have value in themselves.

2. The insurgent group that bids for stocks stipulates that it will accept stocks tendered by shareholders only if a specified total is reached.

3. It's quicker. Shareholders have ten, twenty, or maybe more days within which to tender their stocks. Thus, the insurgents have a clear idea of where they stand.

Public relations professionals are in an excellent position to mobilize resources if the company decides to resist a takeover attempt. If shareholder relations have been properly handled—with an eye toward such contingencies—many answers to the questions and factors listed below would be known. The company's vulnerability to takeovers would be part of the company's on-going monitoring efforts—as would signs that an attempt is being launched. Special communications with shareholders would be built on a strong and sound shareholder relations program. Loyalty to management would not have to be built from scratch but reinforced and drawn upon during the emergency. The concerns and attitudes of shareholders would be known from previous surveys.

Another resource public relations professionals can draw on is support from the financial media and financial community. If the company has been accessible to the media and cooperated in disclosing pertinent information, then it has earned credibility that will lead to greater acceptance of its news releases about the takeover. The same is true of security analysts, brokers, and other members of the financial community.

All of a company's stockholders can be kept informed about a takeover bid and be asked to support the company at a time of crisis. This is a test of goodwill which public relations assiduously tries to build over the years.

Finally, public relations professionals who specialize in investor relations will be familiar with outside specialists who deal with takeovers. These include investment banks, accountants, proxy solicitors, law firms, proxy clerks in brokerage houses, printers, and many others who have to be mobilized quickly for this emergency.

| Fighting Takeovers | Assigned to | Date/Time Assigned | Date/Time Completed |
|---|---|---|---|
| I. With appropriate senior management, establish an on-going program of evaluation and assess your organization as a potential target for acquisition. | _____ | _____ | _____ |
| II. Determine if your company is susceptible to a tender offer, proxy contest, or unwanted merger.<br>  1. Is your company a "bargain" on the stock market?<br>  2. Is your company seductive because of its p/e ratio?<br>  3. What percentage of your company's book value is its stock price?<br>  4. If interest rates go down, can someone pick up your company for less that the liquidation price?<br>  5. Does your company have high liquidity?<br>    a. An excessively high amount of cash on hand?<br>    b. High amount of accounts receivable?<br>  6. Is your company attractive because of a current loss situation? | _____ | _____ | _____ |
| III. Survey your stockholders. What does the latest pulsetaking of your shareholders show?<br>  1. Are they disenchanted, or disinterested, or enthusiastic?<br>  2. What is their attitude toward your:<br>    a. Product line?<br>    b. Management?<br>    c. Company policy?<br>    d. Dividend pay-out? | _____ | _____ | _____ |
| IV. Keep current with all of the above. Check activity on exchanges of your company's stocks. | _____ | _____ | _____ |

*(continued)*

| **Fighting Takeovers** | **Assigned to** | **Date/Time Assigned** | **Date/Time Completed** |
|---|---|---|---|
| V. Read the SEC regulations on tender offers which include exchange of securities. Remember that these regulations provide a company thirty days in which to respond to an offer. | _____ | _____ | _____ |
| VI. Read the Foreign Investment Act. Remember that any foreign investor wanting to acquire more than 5 percent of the company can be stopped by Presidential or SEC order. | _____ | _____ | _____ |
| VII. Establish a standing agreement with a legal firm specializing in proxy contests for quick implementation. Establish an arrangement with a firm of shareholder communications specialists. | _____ | _____ | _____ |
| VIII. Ask your CEO if the company is ready to do battle by:<br>  1. Staggering the board of directors to retain control of the board.<br>  2. Voting new bylaws requiring a 2/3 vote of all shareholders if company management does not want to merger.<br>  3. Checking state laws (where company is incorporated or headquartered) vs. other states for protective statutes for corporations. | _____ | _____ | _____ |
| IX. Prepare a company "emergency plan" in the event of takeover campaign.<br>  1. Is it aggressive enough?<br>  2. Who is in charge?<br>  3. How fast can the defense team be mobilized?<br>  4. When was the plan last updated?<br>  5. Does it fit today's situation?<br>  6. When was the last outside evaluation of the company done?<br>  7. Does the plan mesh with current stock prices? | _____ | _____ | _____ |

*(continued)*

| | Fighting Takeovers | Assigned to | Date/Time Assigned | Date/Time Completed |
|---|---|---|---|---|
| X. | Ask your CEO if top management has alternate companies it would rather merge with as a last resort. Research such companies and their real or apparent relationship to your company. | _____ | _____ | _____ |
| XI. | Prepare a program, besides the annual and interim reports to stockholders, to build investor confidence in the company and its management. | _____ | _____ | _____ |

     1. Is it bold enough?

     2. Is it broad enough?

     3. What proportion of your company's shares are in street name?

     4. Are the company's shares a plaything for fickle institutional investors?

     5. How often does the company write to its stockholders when it is not required to do so?

     6. Has a stockholder survey ever been conducted? Recently?

     7. Does the company communicate with the stockholders in their language?

       a. Many don't know (or care to know) financial jargon or security analysis cant.

       b. Use straight, simple English, but don't be patronizing.

       c. Don't evade tough issues by ducking behind legalese phrasing or tricky words.

     8. Listen to company stockholders:

       a. Answer their letters and calls clearly and promptly.

       b. Give them a chance to ask questions at times other than at the annual meetings, and conduct regional informational meetings.

(continued)

| | Fighting Takeovers | Assigned to | Date/Time Assigned | Date/Time Completed |
|---|---|---|---|---|
| | c. Arrange for the company's transfer agent to forward stockholders' complaints to you promptly. | | | |
| 9. | Determine how many of the stockholders are employees: | | | |
| | a. They need special attention. | | | |
| | b. What about employee investment programs? | | | |
| 10. | Establish a shareholders' participation program. Ask them to assist on some company project or survey. | | | |
| 11. | Determine whether stockholders are getting dividends competitive enough so that they are not inclined to desert the company for another stock. | | | |
| XII. | When an attack is actually imminent, present your story with company reactions to: | _____ | _____ | _____ |
| 1. | Shareholders. | | | |
| 2. | Employees. | | | |
| 3. | Community leaders. | | | |
| 4. | *All* press lists. | | | |
| 5. | Department of Justice. | | | |
| | a. Restraint of trade possibility. | | | |
| | b. Antitrust potential. | | | |
| | c. Monopoly potential. | | | |
| 6. | SEC. | | | |
| 7. | Security analysts. | | | |
| 8. | Congressional bloc. | | | |
| 9. | Distribution or dealer network. | | | |
| 10. | Union leaders. | | | |
| 11. | Special shareholders council (outside). | | | |
| 12. | Outside—proxy specialists. | | | |
| XIII. | Use press conference at three levels: national, regional, and community. | _____ | _____ | _____ |

*(continued)*

| **Fighting Takeovers** | **Assigned to** | **Date/Time Assigned** | **Date/Time Completed** |
|---|---|---|---|
| 1. Set up telephone pyramid using board of directors, employees, dealers, union leaders, community leaders. | | | |
| 2. Use lobbyists or legislative counsel. | | | |
| 3. Maintain a constant stream of new releases on: | | | |
|    a. New facts and happenings. | | | |
|    b. Possible employee changes as a result of proposed take-over. | | | |
|    c. Effect on taxes in plant communities. | | | |
|    d. If applicable, effect on international trade and balance of payments, etc. | | | |
|    e. Industry reaction. | | | |
| 4. Begin a program of advocacy advertising in: | | | |
|    a. The general news media. | | | |
|    b. Financial publications. | | | |
|    c. Plant community media. | | | |
| 5. Consider TV spots with CEO speaking on brief factual material. | | | |

# 37

# SECURITY ANALYSTS, INVESTMENT REPS, A/Es (BROKERAGE) MEETINGS AND INTERVIEWS

What movie critics are to movie-goers, security analysts are to investors. Security analysts are opinion leaders who judge the quality of stocks and bonds. Are a company's securities over- or under-valued on the stock market? Is the recommendation to buy, sell, or hold on? In short, how do researchers see your company's investment in the future?

Security analysts work for various financial institutions that make or offer investment decisions: brokerage houses, banks, insurance companies, investment companies (mutual funds), pension funds, institutional investors, and investment advisory services. They usually specialize in one or more specific industries. Their names and affiliations can be found in directories published by security analyst societies in major cities, e.g., the New York Society of Security Analysts. Most names appear in the membership directory of the Financial Analysts Federation.

In making their investment recommendations—usually accompanied by lengthy reports—security analysts and researchers rely on information they receive from the companies they follow and on their own "investigative reporting" procedures. They look for those "material facts" that influence security prices. They are interested in the guiding philosophy and strategic plans of a company that distinguish it from others in the industry. They particularly want to evaluate that elusive but highly critical factor of managerial ability of the chief executive officer and other top-level managers. For this reason they want to see and talk with management people.

| Security Analysts, Investment Reps, A/Es (Brokerage) Meetings and Interviews | Assigned to | Date/Time Assigned | Date/Time Completed |
|---|---|---|---|
| I. Read the SEC regulations on disclosures relative to individual or mass interviews with security analysts, investment researchers, and banking and brokerage house executives. | _____ | _____ | _____ |
| II. On inquiries from the above, be certain that whatever information is given to an individual is disclosed to everyone *simultaneously*. | _____ | _____ | _____ |
| III. Make all company officers and directors aware of current SEC regulations relative to giving out information of any sort to individuals. Provide a copy of regulations (SEC) and CEO's policy statement. | _____ | _____ | _____ |
| IV. Require that all requests for interviews be submitted through you. | _____ | _____ | _____ |
| V. Become sensitive to the implications of the relationship of company stock prices to new or proposed products, new process or changes, acquisitions, mergers, expansions, closures, lay-offs, etc. | _____ | _____ | _____ |
| VI. In the event of an impending happening, decide on the need for mass disclosure via pertinent product, general circulation, and financial press as well as to security analysts, investment representatives, and account executives.<br><br>1. Because inadvertent disclosures are suspect in the eyes of the SEC, have before you at all times the thought that whatever might affect the status of a company will affect stock prices and be subject to scrutiny by the SEC.<br><br>2. Question every press conference, release, photograph, or utterance in light of this. | _____ | _____ | _____ |

*(continued)*

| Security Analysts, Investment Reps, A/Es (Brokerage) Meetings and Interviews | Assigned to | Date/Time Assigned | Date/Time Completed |
|---|---|---|---|
| VII. Actively solicit opportunities to have your CEO (or designee) speak at a regular meeting of the Society of Security Analysts (locally and in other areas). <br>   1. CEO's speech should include: <br>     a. Company's current health. <br>     b. Predictions—immediate and long-range. <br>     c. Newsworthy or significant items about policies, personnel, and products. <br>   2. Copies of speech should be sent to full financial list immediately. <br>   3. Request Society to invite pertinent news media to the luncheon or dinner meeting. | _____ | _____ | _____ |
| VIII. Use a personal approach with security analysts. Get to know their special informational interests. Keep in touch by phone and through interviews and meetings. Don't waste this opportunity for personal communications. | _____ | _____ | _____ |
| IX. Always direct materials to a specific security analyst. Don't use blind envelopes. Send important material, especially if requested by the security analyst. Some get annoyed when they receive unsolicited, non-personal hand-outs from public relations firms which promote the stocks of client companies. | _____ | _____ | _____ |

# VIII

# SPECIAL EVENTS

Special events are calculated to attract public attention. The chief aim may be to create a newsworthy event for publicity purposes. Another aim may be to use the power of personal media by bringing organizational members in direct contact with one another and outside people.

Event management, as some call it, requires a great deal of imagination to make it exciting and "something to talk about." Whatever concept is developed, it must relate to specific communication objectives. The aim may be to motivate the sales force, to raise employee morale, or to attract media attention to a new product and to build company recognition.

Special events require attention to a myriad of details. Checklists are essential so that every little thing will be done on time. However, it is easy to get so lost in details that the objective of an event is forgotten.

# 38

# EXHIBITS, SHOWS, AND SEMINARS

Increasingly large advertising and publicity budgets and ever more aggressive advertising and editorial claims for products, people, and services, have developed a cocked-eye sophistication and cynicism on the part of the general public.

It is no longer enough to proclaim via full-color advertisements in print and dramatic commercials on TV and radio that your new wonder drug will cure practically everything wrong with mankind, or that there has been a break-through in science which has resulted in an idiot-proof gadget that will enable a driver to get fifty miles per gallon and simultaneously cut home-heating bills by not less than 50 percent.

There is a rapidly growing desire—even need—to see the product with one's own eyes; to watch it achieve its purpose; to try to work the new cleaning device, or whatever. Hence, the burgeoning interest by organizations in expanded, cost-efficient exhibits and displays, as well as in the opportunities available through the medium of seminars with their concomitant papers, publicity, and displays.

It is a mistake to imagine that the organization that spends the most money for an exhibit, trade show, or convention hall will benefit the most. Throwing money at the problem without full analysis and preparation is a total waste. The DPR must combat the well-intentioned pressures of marketing departments and other special interests.

The DPR also must avoid the Barnum Syndrome with its obvious allure. Strobe lights, flamboyant day-glow and amplified music may make visitors look, but they also make them turn away. Leggy, scantily clad, pretty models who parrot incomprehensible (to them) technical product claims do not do much for any product, service, or organization that imagines that this approach is an avenue to profit or prestige.

Probably the most important decision that will be made by the DPR in assessing his or her organization's exhibit efforts will be the determination of its purpose and target. All other considerations are subordinate to this; the budget, the size of space rented for the exhibit, the type of exhibit, and the manpower necessary to accomplish the goal are all subsidiary matters.

Main purposes of any exhibit and show are generally distinct but not discrete; there are usually combination goals with major and minor targets. For example, if the main purpose is to be one of recruitment, there must of necessity be an ancillary effort at corporate or organizational prestige. Obversely, should the principal purpose of the exhibit be that of enhancing the prestige of the organization, recruitment is definitely implied.

A visit to any trade show or convention's exhibit hall quickly shows the changing character of the exhibitor attitude as well as the physical display and its operation. Today, these are major events with participation by senior organizational personnel. The exhibits have long ago dropped the atmosphere of a once-a-year medicine show with attendant brouhaha. Obviously, there are still and will continue to be crowd-pullers, such as give-aways or free samples or prize drawings, but these too have become more imaginative. Do not over-react and become so reticent that no one comes to your exhibit to see what you want them to see.

It is not necessary to have the largest exhibit booth in the show (unless your product or service size warrants it). What is necessary is a display that is attractive enough to get visitors to stop; one that makes clear its purpose immediately and imaginatively. It should be easily accessible (can they come in and walk around or sit down?) and well-staffed by friendly people at all times. The display and its signs must be neither patronizing nor exotic. There must be an adequate supply of take-aways and the space must be kept immaculate.

What is desired is an attitude and display that one would feel comfortable with in one's own home.

After the show, convention, or seminar, an audit of the organization's participation must be made as to effectiveness, cost, and achievement, together with attendants' suggestions for improvement for the next exhibit.

| Exhibits, Shows, and Seminars | Assigned to | Date/Time Assigned | Date/Time Completed |
|---|---|---|---|
| I. Assess company budget for exhibitions and shows and determine its realism. | _____ | _____ | _____ |
| II. Have a cost analysis done for each proposed show. | _____ | _____ | _____ |
|    1. Determine cost of space. | | | |
|    2. Estimate number of employees, both in preparation and staffing. Figure their costs. | | | |
|    3. Estimate cost of exhibit materials and other preparation costs. | | | |
|    4. Check out costs of professional exhibit specialists. | | | |
|    5. Check all division/department heads for their estimates of values received by having company participation in each show. | | | |
| III. Assess effects on company's sales, reputation, new business, recruitment, etc., if any show is dropped from schedule. Estimate effect of smaller exhibit and space in costs and results. | _____ | _____ | _____ |
| IV. Assign PR staff to cover show. | _____ | _____ | _____ |
|    1. Get report on legitimacy of company participation. | | | |
|    2. Review guest book or other list of those who see your exhibit. | | | |
|    3. Check your advertising department for special ads concomitant with the show. | | | |
|    4. Be sure that you have enough PR staff to man booth and hospitality suite. | | | |
| V. Determine show/exhibit target: | _____ | _____ | _____ |
|    1. Recruiting. | | | |
|    2. Sales. | | | |
|    3. Prestige. | | | |
|    4. "Showing the flag." | | | |
|    5. Dealer relationships and participation. | | | |
|    6. Platform for new product announcement. | | | |

*(continued)*

| | Exhibits, Shows, and Seminars | Assigned to | Date/Time Assigned | Date/Time Completed |
|---|---|---|---|---|
| | 7. Demonstration of "state of the art" and company status in advances. | | | |
| | 8. Springboard for sales meeting. | | | |
| VI. | Check news releases appropriate to the show. Save a significant release timed for show period. | _____ | _____ | _____ |
| VII. | Determine who is to be responsible for the hospitality suite. | _____ | _____ | _____ |
| | 1. Make certain that someone opens and closes and supplies the suite. | | | |
| | 2. Watch out for "freeloaders" and arrange for legitimate admission system. | | | |
| | 3. Make certain that there are available visual aids, samples, press kits, news releases, promotional literature, company annual reports, etc. | | | |
| VIII. | Decide how leads will be solicited at the exhibit. Make sure they are followed up after the show (within five days). | _____ | _____ | _____ |
| IX. | If seminars are to be held in conjunction with the show, get list of those who will read papers. | _____ | _____ | _____ |
| | 1. Read the papers yourself before the show to determine the significance of the releases. | | | |
| | 2. Prepare appropriate news releases about the papers and those who will read them. | | | |
| X. | Submit a re-cap or summary of the show and your company's participation to pertinent division/department heads and the CEO. | _____ | _____ | _____ |
| | 1. Include your reaction. | | | |
| | 2. Get reactions of showgoers (quotes). | | | |
| | 3. Assess cost effectiveness. | | | |
| | 4. Include recommendations for improvement for future shows. | | | |

# 39

# COMPANY DINNERS
# AND BASHES

Excluding a labor crisis, there is no company occurrence of a routine nature that is more talked about—and for a longer period—than the "Company Dinner" and/or "The Outing."

It is both eagerly and apprehensively anticipated. The most eager are the families of the employees who, only once or twice each year, have a chance to meet and talk to those about whom the spouses talk a great deal, and also to meet other company families. The apprehension is usually prevalent among those (public relations staff) who must prepare and conduct the affair.

These affairs are generally the only time that management meets with all employees, more or less amicably, without the giving or taking of orders. And it is at these times that enlightened management strengthens a "family" loyalty, takes the opportunity to build pride of association and achievement, finds it possible to correct misunderstandings, and develops new dimensions among all employees at all levels. The annual company dinner and the summer outing is a "show case" for management and must be considered a challenge rather than an obligatory bore.

It is not without reason that top-rank executives who have had a chance to study the success and motivations of Japanese industry, all comment admiringly of the organizational loyalty and family relationship embraced by Japanese workers and managers, and in companies of all sizes. They realize that such successes are not just robotics, but are basically human relationships.

The apprehension felt by experienced public relations persons is not without justification when it comes to any sort of company affair where "hourly-paid" employees eat and drink with their supervisors and managers.

There is a warm ambience, people calling each other by their first names, a few too many drinks, and the gates of inhibition collapse. PR staffers must watch for those who see a chance to "show that twerp from the A Department," those who experience an irresistible burst of machismo, and those who, having "always admired the ad manager's secretary" in discreet silence, mistake the dance floor for the entrance to a bedroom.

It is the PR staff which will be responsible for firmness and tact in dealing with such situations. Act quickly and with decision is the word of those experienced in such matters in removing trouble makers from the site.

Christmas parties have become a cliché for embarassing confrontations, both romantic and bellicose. In some organizations the Christmas Party has been dropped as a company affair as a result of out-of-hand situations. Preparedness, alertness, and quick action are the operational words for the PR staff at any company affair.

Each organization has a specific set of problems in staging its company dinner or outing. One firm may invite all employee children. If so, arrangements must be made in advance for their accommodation. Another company may have a policy of having its annual affair at an out-of-town plant, in which case transportation will be the big problem. There are many variants, but the following checklist is a common denominator.

| Company Dinners and Bashes | Assigned to | Date/Time Assigned | Date/Time Completed |
|---|---|---|---|
| I. In choosing a location, be certain that:<br>1. It is convenient for all.<br>2. It is large enough.<br>3. It has a controllable bar.<br>4. It will be comfortable for all. | _____ | _____ | _____ |
| II. There will be control over impromptu romantic, impassioned, or belligerent situations. | _____ | _____ | _____ |
| III. There will be sufficient food, and that it will be served on time. | _____ | _____ | _____ |
| IV. Specific hours are set for the affair. | _____ | _____ | _____ |
| V. One person will be responsible for giving orders to hotel or establishment personnel. | _____ | _____ | _____ |
| VI. One person will be responsible for handling the entertainment. | _____ | _____ | _____ |
| VII. There are personnel assigned as "sergeants-at-arms." | _____ | _____ | _____ |
| VIII. There is proper accommodation for checking and parking. | _____ | _____ | _____ |
| IX. Someone will be in charge of emergency situations (e.g., firefighters, nurses, etc.). | _____ | _____ | _____ |
| X. Proper I.D.'s are used (badges) to eliminate crashers and freeloaders. | _____ | _____ | _____ |
| XI. Determine whether the affair will be for or limited to:<br>1. Direct employees or including employees' families.<br>2. Customers or good friends of the company.<br>3. Directors.<br>4. Principal shareholders.<br>5. External service personnel.<br>   a. Advertising agency.<br>   b. Law firm. | _____ | _____ | _____ |

*(continued)*

| **Company Dinners and Bashes** | Assigned to | Date/Time Assigned | Date/Time Completed |
|---|---|---|---|
|    c.  Contractors. | | | |
|    d.  PR counsel. | | | |
|    e.  Brokerage house. | | | |
|    f.  Community leaders. | | | |
|   6.  Press. | | | |
|   7.  Company photographer. | | | |
| XII.  Assign a staff person to assure attendance of CEO, president, chairperson, senior officers, and to: | _____ | _____ | _____ |
|   1.  Provide a "ready room" for head table guests and bring them in all together. | | | |
|   2.  Provide lectern and microphone(s) for head table. | | | |
|   3.  Signal for speech time to coincide with dessert eating. | | | |
|   4.  Allow no table clearing until end of speeches. | | | |
|   5.  Make certain speeches are not too long. | | | |
|   6.  If necessary, provide speech hand-outs to press table. | | | |
| XIII.  In addition to above, summer outings should have these considerations: | _____ | _____ | _____ |
|   1.  Determine method of assuring employee family attendance and participation in events. | | | |
|   2.  Be sure park is large enough and has facilities for proper summer events (ball games, etc.). | | | |
|   3.  Be certain safety factors are under control. | | | |
|   4.  Assign one person to handle each of the following: | | | |
|    a.  Food. | | | |
|    b.  Bar. | | | |
|    c.  Athletic programs. | | | |
|    d.  Children's events. | | | |

*(continued)*

| Company Dinners and Bashes | Assigned to | Date/Time Assigned | Date/Time Completed |
|---|---|---|---|
| e. Entertainment.<br>f. Prizes and awards.<br>g. Transportation for those without cars.<br>h. Transportation for those who should not drive home. | | | |
| XIV. Assign a company photographer and *employee publication or company writer* to prepare promo for distribution within the company.<br>1. Instruct photographer to be sure to get at least one photo of each person attending, preferably while participating in an event.<br>2. Arrange for free, or minimal cost, prints for employees.<br>3. Plan to produce a broadside of a montage of the best photos and distribute them to all employees and other selected groups (shareholders, local papers, etc.) | _____ | _____ | _____ |

# 40

# PLANT TOURS

A survey of plant tour guides made a few years ago revealed that there were four inevitable remarks made by residents of municipalities where plant facilities were located. In no particular order they were:

**1.** "I couldn't imagine what you did in here."

**2.** "Oh. So that's how you make them."

**3.** "I never realized it was so complicated."

**4.** "I didn't know you made those."

Obviously, there is a deep well of curiosity about the inside, the workings, and the workers of any plant on the part of the residents in that community. Families of workers also have an urge to know and see the actual place and how Dad, or Mom, or Sis, or Brother works.

Too, among the fondest and most humorous memories of elementary school activities are those dealing with trips and tours of places where things are produced.

Some organizations capitalize on this curiosity to good advantage with formal, periodic tours. These well-organized tour patterns are carefully designed to provide visitors with the most interesting aspects of the production without interfering in production activities. Tour guides are hired especially for the task and receive thorough training in answering questions about the company, its products, policies, and personnel.

Some companies have provided tour literature for take-aways, which give the organization a second effect benefit of the tour. Others arrange for samples of products in small or miniature-sized packages. Still other companies give each visitor an actual piece of an uncommon substance used in the fabrication of the product. In some cases, visitors have even received individual packages of the product with their names printed on the outside. In any case, the tour should be a memorable one, leaving the visitor with good feelings about the company.

Once an organization decides to offer tours of its facilities, it should be marketed as one would market a product or service. An aggressive search should be made for individuals and groups who might be interested in taking such a tour. Invitations should be sent to teachers, managers, secretaries, etc. Publicizing the visits through local newspapers, the company paper, local radio and TV stations, all add to the feeling of goodwill. Notifying the Chamber of Commerce or the Board of Trade that visitors are welcome at specific times and dates will often result in requests from out-of-towners, thus adding to the company's visibility.

In addition to recruiting guides from departments from within the company, some companies hire guides from the outside who then receive full training on facts about the company. Many of these guides are "moonlighting" teachers, firefighters, college students on summer vacation, police officers, and CETA workers. Applicants for the job should be personable, patient, and have a strong desire to help people understand.

When employee family groups make tours, it is worthwhile allowing the relevant employee to accompany the tour.

| **Plant Tours** | **Assigned to** | **Date/Time Assigned** | **Date/Time Completed** |
|---|---|---|---|
| I. Consider establishing a regular program of plant tours. | _____ | _____ | _____ |
| II. "Isolate" specific areas of interest for the purpose of such tours. | _____ | _____ | _____ |
| III. Visit and inspect the tour site to mark the limits, lines, and length of the tour. | _____ | _____ | _____ |
| IV. Obtain permission and agreement from pertinent area manager. Check pertinent employee reaction to proposed tour. | _____ | _____ | _____ |
| V. Identify target audiences (visitors); i.e., schools, clubs, stockholders, visiting dealers, congressional blocs, other VIP's, trade press. Invite other employees and their families for a first tour. | _____ | _____ | _____ |
| VI. Recruit guides for the tour from the lower management levels and train them for the task. Write out the tour pattern and have it approved by relevant executives. The final pattern should be memorized by the guides. | _____ | _____ | _____ |
| VII. Set days and times so there is no interference with production.<br>  1. Prepare stanchions, ribbons, and signs of identification and directions. These become the responsibility of the department from which the guides are recruited.<br>  2. Spot and place directions and signs well before visitors arrive.<br>  3. Keep groups to a manageable size, preferably to between twelve and fifteen.<br>  4. Prepare and distribute a small printed take-away flyer to each visitor, including other mementos where appropriate. These hand-outs are excellent vehicles for company publicity. | _____ | _____ | _____ |

*(continued)*

| Plant Tours | Assigned to | Date/Time Assigned | Date/Time Completed |
|---|---|---|---|
| VIII. Consider conveniences for people taking tours:<br>1. Parking.<br>2. Lunch or refreshments, restrooms (especially for groups).<br>3. Reception area away from the front door, and near a coat-check area.<br>4. Security arrangements to prevent unnecessary incursions, wandering, snooping, and theft. | —— | —— | —— |
| IX. Provide badges or name tags for the guests.<br>1. Provide identification tags for the guides.<br>2. Place signs over machinery or work in progress. Make them simple and explicit. | —— | —— | —— |
| X. Distribute press releases with photos immediately to pertinent media.<br>1. Arrange for Polaroid shots of guests, and give to them.<br>2. Give employees copies.<br>3. Give copies to company paper. | —— | —— | —— |
| XI. Consider sponsoring an essay contest for school groups. This would include what was seen on the tour. Give a prize to the winner of the best essay. | —— | —— | —— |
| XII. Write a "thank you" letter to each group leader. | —— | —— | —— |
| XIII. In case of full tours of entirely new facilities, i.e., new or expanded buildings:<br>1. Give employees and their families a special tour before outside groups have visited.<br>2. Invite community neighbors and leaders and the press second.<br>3. The third group should consist of security analysts, investment group members, and stockholders.<br>4. Dealers and customers should be asked fourth. | —— | —— | —— |

# 41

# INDUSTRY PARTICIPATION

In today's political ambience with the impact of pressure groups and special interest pleadings, no single organization, unless it has an almost unlimited budget and a near-religious dedication to a specific cause, can have enough clout to be effective.

It would be impossible for any legislature, or the public as a whole, to listen to the scores of thousands of individual voices, each representing an individual organization. Practicality dictates the need for spokesmen for common cause groups; a single voice to state the case for thousands.

There is, then, a necessity to join industry, professional, and trade associations. But one's organization must be more than just a dues-paying member. Active, even aggressive, participation is called for, with support necessary to give input and muscle into the association so that its considered statement will be listened to.

There have long been industry and professional groups that have provided legislative counsel or lobbyists. Although many of these have been extremely powerful, that one activity seems to have been the extent of the group effort. Enlightened industry has recognized that that was not enough; that to present its case fairly, it must not only rely on a paid lobbyist, but must itself put in time and thought to provide a multi-faceted program if it is to gain dimension and acceptance.

Even those groups considered to be single-purposed and of a closed mind to any concept but its own, have begun to see the need for other means and methods, for new avenues and approaches, and to gain access to the over-crowded ears of legislatures and various publics.

Today's management is aware that participation by any organization, in the efforts of its industry, professional or trade association, must spread across all management levels, and, indeed, filter throughout the entire employee roster where possible or feasible.

Significant impact on the public (and on law makers) is gained, not through the "quick fix" of financial support by a political action committee (PAC) only, but with the substantial power evidenced when all segments and personnel begin saying the same things in the same language. This does not mean the obsolete system of mailing thousands of identical post-cards from all over the country to a congressional subcommittee. That is recognized for what it is. But when a well-known scientist speaks to peers at a seminar; or when a parade is held by 10,000 "hard hats"; or when original letters appear in daily papers throughout the country; or when a major symphony orchestra's program is telecast, interspersed with simple, direct messages; or when a CEO of a national company makes provocative statements on a national TV panel; or even when schools, classes, or camps for young people begin to teach the proper method of achieving a common goal spring up, then the public becomes aware of an industry or profession or group trying to communicate its message.

It is assumed that the purpose of any such participation is ethical, moral, and sincerely for the common good. The activities of lobbying, PAC support, boycotting, etc., by the "anti's," the fringe organization with wild-eyed zealots, the seemingly logical hypocrites with selfish goals, all carry within them their own poison of self-destruction. Their target soon becomes skeptical and turns away, while the campaigns for the benefit of the greater public eventually succeeds.

Active participation in associations representing groups of similar organizations carry the responsibility to monitor goals, strategies, and tactics. Keep all these as clean as you would those of your own organization—set your personal ethics as the criterion.

In approaching any organization's participation in group efforts, the first and most important step is analysis. Determining the need and extent of activities will establish the size of the budget, the manpower, and usually the procedure and methodology. The proposed programs must be viewed as at least as significant to the long-range viability of the organization as any advertising, marketing, or public relations efforts.

| Industry Participation | Assigned to | Date/Time Assigned | Date/Time Completed |
|---|---|---|---|
| I. Make an inventory of the professional trade and scientific groups your organization and its people belong to. | _____ | _____ | _____ |
| II. Check the degree of participation in each of these organizations, but do not list those in which you are only a dues-paying member. | _____ | _____ | _____ |
| III. List your organization's participation in conventions, shows, exhibitions, seminars, or other activities. | _____ | _____ | _____ |
| IV. Investigate the need and cost effectiveness of your employees' attendance at such affairs (in addition to those in which you are operating exhibits and displays). | _____ | _____ | _____ |
| V. Determine whether your company maintains a proper incentive program and budget for company employee-authors to write, submit, or read papers at these affairs or in their publications. | _____ | _____ | _____ |
| VI. Establish a program for collating and reprinting in hard cover, an annual collection of employee-written articles, papers, and speeches for distribution to:<br>1. Employees.<br>2. Authors' suggested list.<br>3. Customers.<br>4. Potential market areas.<br>5. Appropriate news media. | _____ | _____ | _____ |
| VII. Establish a special budget for building displays and exhibits for various organizational affairs.<br>1. Plan ancillary use of these materials in community affairs.<br>2. Arrange for news release of photos of attractive or ingenious displays, exhibits, or models developed by your advertising department. | _____ | _____ | _____ |
| VIII. Set up a small budget for advertising in programs of conventions, shows, etc. Get your publicity department to capitalize on these. | _____ | _____ | _____ |

*(continued)*

| Industry Participation | Assigned to | Date/Time Assigned | Date/Time Completed |
|---|---|---|---|
| IX. Have all speeches planned for delivery at conventions, seminars, panels, etc., submitted to you for corporate awareness. Arrange for news release of significant speech material at the time of delivery at shows. | _____ | _____ | _____ |
| X. Establish a program for your CEO to comment on in writing for the authors of the speeches. Capitalize further on such speeches by distribution to:<br>1. Shareholders.<br>2. Customers.<br>3. Security analysts.<br>4. Hometown newspapers.<br>5. Alumni publications.<br>6. Corporate advertising when relevant. | _____ | _____ | _____ |
| XI. Investigate the advantages of acting in concert with other organizations within your industry, society, association, etc., in lobbying matters.<br>1. Support a legislative counsel for the industry in Washington.<br>2. Use some of this lobbying material in your corporate advertising.<br>3. Issue news releases from industry lobbying material with attribution to a company officer. | _____ | _____ | _____ |
| XII. Determine the specific company person who is prepared to testify for the industry at congressional hearings, and its impact on:<br>1. Employment.<br>2. GNP.<br>3. Trade deficit.<br>4. Market position versus foreign interests.<br>5. Obtain approval from industry for pre-release of such material.<br>6. Be prepared for follow-up by news media, then speak to the regional and local impact. | _____ | _____ | _____ |

# 42

# MAKE OR BUY: IN-HOUSE OR OUTSIDE SUPPLIERS

Because public relations itself is a service activity, rather than a production effort, there has long been a controversy over whether to make or buy such services and service supplies. Obviously, there is no set standard as to which is the best system, as there are no two organizations exactly alike. Most companies arrive at their best working arrangement by empiricism. Generally, senior management will accept the decision reached by the DPR when he or she points out the cost and quality effectiveness factors.

There are about two dozen different kinds of services and service supplies that are used in making any public relations department a successful working staff activity. Each of these can be either an in-house capability or an outside supplier.

In analyzing the various items on such an inventory, the DPR must, with the approval of the CEO, determine the size and capabilities of a proposed staff. If he or she decides that one can show viability in hiring permanent staff to accomplish all of the necessary services, then there is no question as to make or buy. Or the DPR and the CEO may decide that it is best for the organization to maintain only a supervisory capability on the permanent payroll, and to buy all outside services. Again, there is no problem to solve. But in most cases, the system that works out best will be a combination of the two: a basic staff and the use of outside services suppliers.

Most of the items on the laundry list of needs for the well-working PR department quickly fall into either category: internal or external. Generally, it is far more efficient to use a clipping service rather than subscribing to hundreds of publications and having staff members spend costly hours reading through them looking for items about one's firm. Similarly, the DPR finds it considerably less costly, generally, to employ a company that specializes in building displays and exhibits, rather than hiring a staff of carpenters, designers, artists, painters, electricians, etc.

It is normally considered wise to hire a "stringer" photographer to get the necessary photographs at a facility a thousand miles away, instead of sending out a staff camera person, with all the attendant expenses, to shoot a single picture.

Most organizations do not make their own TV commercials but rely on specialists in that field to do the job. So, too, do most companies find it cost and quality effective to employ an advertising agency, although there are many good internal or house agencies.

There is nothing in any company rules that requires a decision of the DPR to hire outside services or supply them from his or her own staff, to be a permanent thing. Changes can and will be made in such decisions.

| Make Or Buy: (In-House or Outside Suppliers) | Assigned to | Date/Time Assigned | Date/Time Completed |
|---|---|---|---|
| I. Prepare a list of suppliers and services. | _____ | _____ | _____ |
| II. Run a cost and quality analysis on each of the above. | _____ | _____ | _____ |
| III. The basic list of required services includes: | _____ | _____ | _____ |

    1. Surveys.
    2. Research.
    3. Computers.
    4. Photography.
    5. Artwork.
    6. Printing.
    7. Clipping services.
    8. Mailing lists.
    9. Mailing, production, and distribution.
   10. Displays and exhibits.
   11. Packaging.
   12. Advertising.
   13. Material services.
   14. Photo stringers.
      a. Domestic primary, secondary, and tertiary markets.
      b. Plant communities.
      c. Multinational cities.
   15. Writer stringers.
      a. Domestic primary, secondary, and tertiary markets.
      b. Plant communities.
      c. Multinational cities.
   16. Syndicates.
   17. Lecture or speakers' bureaus.
   18. Videotape and film.
   19. Book publishers.
   20. Sales promotion devices such as contests, mail-aways.
   21. PR—on-going or special projects.
   22. Publicity services—special projects.

*(continued)*

| **Make Or Buy:** (In-House or Outside Suppliers) | Assigned to | Date/Time Assigned | Date/Time Completed |
|---|---|---|---|
| IV. Consider these factors: | ——— | ——— | ——— |

IV. Consider these factors:
1. Outline the economic options.
2. Study the employee impact.
3. Expect full implementation.
4. Decide on central in-house programs vs. regional or plant resident PR.
5. Investigate whether your company policy requires or prohibits in-house capability or only decision-making at senior level.
6. Determine relationship of each of these with the other as to priority, seniority, etc.
7. Determine the responsible person for each of the segments.
8. Consider a combination of some in-house and outside services after considering in-house availability.
9. Consider the benefits of group account executive supervisors for different facets of the company for individual or groups of these segments.
10. Consider making an autonomous subsidiary for any or all of these.
11. Determine and implement the Most Efficacious Method (MEM).

## Notes

# SOCIAL RESPONSIBILITY

Managers are no longer judged solely by their ability to maximize profits. They are beginning to recognize that it is also important to upgrade the quality of life. The formation of social responsibility committees by boards of directors of large corporations is a sign that non-economic factors must be considered in modern decision making.

**DIMENSIONS OF SOCIAL RESPONSIBILITY** The concern for the broad impact of an organization on society has many dimensions. The chief among these are:

1. Responsibly fulfilling a company's primary function of producing goods and services needed by society. In performing this economic role, a company also provides jobs—both directly by employing a work force and indirectly by stimulating the economy through its payroll and purchases of materials and services.

**2.** Recognizing social costs and attempting to reduce or compensate for them. Social costs refer to air and water pollution, endangering employee health and safety, and creating other real costs of producing and selling goods that are not recorded in a company's accounting system. Government regulations such as the Clean Air Act increasingly compel business to reduce social costs. Nevertheless, companies can voluntarily exercise initiative by going beyond legal requirements or acting before being legally required to do so.

**3.** Making social investments through corporate contributions and sponsorship of projects and programs that add to the infrastructure of society. A healthier, better educated community ultimately helps everyone.

**4.** Helping to solve social problems that affect business or that business can solve more efficiently than government.

Making donations and contributions is a major way corporations have addressed many dimensions of social responsibility. Traditionally, individual business people have made contributions out of feelings of generosity. Now corporations have largely assumed the task of charitable giving by business.

The modern approach to corporate giving is to view it as a social investment rather than an act of benevolence. In Irving Kristol's words, corporate giving is a form of "useful philanthropy." He gives the example of mining concerns giving money to engineering schools because they recruit from them. Other kinds of social investments need not be on a quid pro quo basis but a payment to maintain and build the communities in which a company's offices and plants are located.

Private enterprise is often better equipped and more efficient than government in dealing with many of society's problems—training the hardcore unemployed, analyzing a city's traffic problems, rehabilitating housing, helping black entrepreneurship, etc. When corporations do not undertake such programs on a purely profit basis, a social responsibility element is present.

**NEED FOR PHILOSOPHY** Each company must develop its own philosophy of corporate philanthropy based on the scope described above. The trend is to avoid making capricious decisions. As management applies the MBO (management by objectives) approach to all decisions, public relations programs must be supported by a convincing cost-effectiveness rationale. Cost-effectiveness criteria will also be applied.

Public affairs considerations increasingly influence the philosophy of social responsibility. Corporate philanthropy is designed to strengthen and preserve the private sector against further encroachment by government. This means that private institutions must be kept solvent and kept from becoming excessively dependent on government grants and contracts. Some companies furthermore believe that corporations should not support colleges and universities whose faculty denounce the capitalistic system.

**SOCIAL ACCOUNTING** Ultimately, corporate survival depends on society's evaluation of total corporate performance—social as well as economic. A few companies have experimented with social audits. These attempt to enumerate and measure all the ways in which a company benefits and harms a society. Most audits don't go further than the publication of a social report which describes a company's various social programs. Little or no attention is paid to measurement.

# 43

# DONATIONS AND CONTRIBUTIONS

How much to give and to whom are typical questions faced by business firms. Whether to give is a Scrooge-like question few companies now bother to ask. Business is expected to keep nonprofit organizations alive because they are part of the infrastructure upon which business depends.

**SIZE OF VOLUNTARY SECTOR** The voluntary sector is a large and vital part of American society. *Giving in America,* a report of the Commission on Private Philanthropy and Public Needs, gives some estimates of its dimensions. There are six million voluntary organizations in the United States employing one of ten service workers and one of six professional workers. They cover religion, education, health, social welfare, the arts, humanities, and other public enterprises.

Individual contributions account for over 90 percent of private contributions. About 50 percent of corporate contributions have in recent years come from fewer than 1000 companies with assets of $200 million or more. It's these large companies that have been examining the rationale for giving most closely.

**RATIONALE FOR GIVING** A pro-active approach is replacing the wait-for-requests attitude which still predominates. Companies seek to support voluntary organizations that somehow tie in with a company's presence in a community. The rationale may be to counterbalance social costs and to improve the business climate and the quality of life of the community.

Many companies use the general guideline of giving about one percent of pre-tax profits. The Internal Revenue Code allows companies to give up to 5 percent, so the inclination of public policy is clear: Corporations should give more. The Filer Commission recommends that corporations give 2 percent of pre-tax earnings. With cutbacks in government grants to the arts and social programs, some business people have urged corporations to help fill the gap.

When the corporate income tax rate is 46 percent, the government indirectly pays that amount. This has led some corporate statesmen to query: Don't we have enough faith in ourselves to believe that we can better decide how to spend this money than government? As government tries to reduce its involvement in the private sector, corporations may indeed be pressured to increase their giving.

| Donations and Contributions | Assigned to | Date/Time Assigned | Date/Time Completed |
|---|---|---|---|
| I. Arrange for an annual meeting among plant managers, division managers, personnel manager, marketing vice president, treasurer, CEO, and chairperson to determine the gross pool amount to be given away in a variety of outlets. If the dollar amount is significant as a percentage of profit, decide if it should be announced publicly, or if it should remain internal for political reasons. | _____ | _____ | _____ |
| II. Compile a list of all possible and probable demanding organizations by officials designated at the meeting to handle contributions and donations. | _____ | _____ | _____ |
| III. Determine what proportion or which categories headquarters should handle and which divisions should be designated as having discretionary funds, and how much to each (percentage and dollar amount). | _____ | _____ | _____ |
| IV. Discuss the pragmatic effects and reactions, and analyze these relative to categorical awards. For example, if you give to the Catholic Church, can you turn down the Baptists in each community? | _____ | _____ | _____ |
| V. Determine how far down the list the company should go—whether at the executive office or plant level, i.e., what is the cut-off for categories? | _____ | _____ | _____ |
| VI. Determine how much support should go to local vs. regional vs. national, and the proportion to each. | _____ | _____ | _____ |
| VII. Consider the frequency of the donation—is it one-time giving or a monthly pledge? | _____ | _____ | _____ |
| VIII. Decide whether awards (scholarships) should be included in the donation funds. | _____ | _____ | _____ |

(continued)

| Donations and Contributions | Assigned to | Date/Time Assigned | Date/Time Completed |
|---|---|---|---|
| IX. Explore the possibility of contributing services or products vis-à-vis cash, or a combination of resources. | \_\_\_\_\_ | \_\_\_\_\_ | \_\_\_\_\_ |
| X. Know the difference between a normal donation and the emerging need for a societal donation. | \_\_\_\_\_ | \_\_\_\_\_ | \_\_\_\_\_ |
| XI. Discuss and decide whether the donation should be to one "umbrella" organization, such as the United Way, or to smaller, independent organizations. Determine which members of the "umbrella" organization should receive the funds. | \_\_\_\_\_ | \_\_\_\_\_ | \_\_\_\_\_ |
| XII. Explore and decide whether the company should adopt an individual cause and contribute a major portion of production dollars to that cause on either a temporary or permanent basis. | \_\_\_\_\_ | \_\_\_\_\_ | \_\_\_\_\_ |
| XIII. Design a policy for employee donations by payroll deductions. | \_\_\_\_\_ | \_\_\_\_\_ | \_\_\_\_\_ |
| XIV. Discuss in detail the self-interest aspect vis-à-vis the "moral obligations" of the company. | \_\_\_\_\_ | \_\_\_\_\_ | \_\_\_\_\_ |

# 44

# SPONSORSHIPS

One of the most direct and visible ways of enhancing the quality of life of citizens is sponsorship of events and programs of interest to them. Mobil's sponsorship of "Masterpiece Theater," for example, has enriched the lives of many television viewers. Sponsorship of community-based symphony concerts has exposed more people to music and stimulated future interest in the symphony. Corporate sponsorship of art exhibits has particularly been popular.

**BENEFITS TO BUSINESS**

Business benefits from sponsorships in these ways:

► Heightens visibility of the company.
► Associates the corporate image with humanistic values.
► Attracts high calibre employees to companies located in culturally rich communities.
► Helps retention of employees who appreciate the improved quality of community life.

Most companies are no longer shy about seeking media exposure for their sponsorships. Recipient organizations help by giving credit in their news releases. The Metropolitan Museum of Art and the Museum of Modern Art have included a specific request in their press materials that editors credit corporate sponsors.

**GIFT-MATCHING** A new development in sponsorships is gift-matching programs for cultural institutions. The idea is borrowed from the practice of major corporations to match their employees' gifts to educational institutions with equal donations from the corporation. This system gives employees a voice and solves the problem of turning down groups. They can always be told: "If you can get any of our employees to give, we will match the donation."

As the checklist shows, there are many other kinds of sponsorships than cultural activities. Whatever interests employees, customers, and neighbors can be added to the list.

| **Sponsorships** | **Assigned to** | **Date/Time Assigned** | **Date/Time Completed** |
|---|---|---|---|
| I. Initiate new areas of sponsorship; each is an opportunity to capitalize on inexpensive ways to create good community relations and to gain prestige. Some groups that a company might help to sponsor are:<br>1. Little League teams.<br>2. Bowling teams.<br>3. Tennis tournaments.<br>4. Horse/dog shows.<br>5. Essay and crafts contests.<br>6. Presentations of annual trophies and cups.<br>7. Marching bands. | _____ | _____ | _____ |
| II. Consider putting company name on T-shirts/uniforms. | _____ | _____ | _____ |
| III. Consider using matching funds solicitations for:<br>1. Museum special exhibits.<br>2. Sending marching bands or teams to national contests and/or parades.<br>3. Use of company aircraft or road vehicle for transporting teams or special-case person.<br>4. Musical marathons, auctions, etc., for fundraising for orchestras, etc. | _____ | _____ | _____ |
| IV. Watch for opportunities to sponsor telecasts and broadcasts of national events emanating from local areas. | _____ | _____ | _____ |
| V. Make possible the telecast or broadcast of symphony concerts:<br>1. Major symphony orchestra on PBS networks.<br>2. Selected stations for community or school symphony orchestra.<br>3. Choruses.<br>4. Chamber music. | _____ | _____ | _____ |

*(continued)*

| Sponsorships | Assigned to | Date/Time Assigned | Date/Time Completed |
|---|---|---|---|
| VI. Decide on an equitable policy—and be consistent in staying with it—of advertising in programs for local events (school, church, football, etc.). | _____ | _____ | _____ |
| VII. Keep separate your donation/contribution program from any sponsorships. | _____ | _____ | _____ |
| VIII. Evaluate a corporate policy for budgeting discretionary funds for plant or facility managers to use for sponsoring purely local events. National-impact events, affairs, contests, etc., must be the responsibility of the DPR. | _____ | _____ | _____ |

# 45

# FUND-RAISING ASSISTANCE

Chief executive officers of major corporations in communties typically lead fund-raising drives. Their involvement symbolizes the spirit of voluntarism which is an essential part of American life. The Filer Commission estimates that nearly six billion womanhours and manhours of volunteer work were contributed to nonprofit organizations in 1973. The value of these in-kind contributions equalled that of individual money contributions.

Many corporations encourage rank-and-file as well as managerial employees to do meaningful community work. Employee publications are used to recognize these contributions. Some companies go further and expect their managers to join community organizations and play an active role in them.

Sometimes business attempts to influence the policies of community groups for the purpose of instilling business values. For example, businessmen have been urged to become hospital trustees so that they could "insist on bottom line discipline" and question such decisions as the purchase of expensive new equipment.

All organizations should take an inventory of their resources to see which can be made available to meet community needs. Companies have encouraged some of their scientists to lecture in school science classes, and some have volunteered their financial experts to help work out town and city budgets. Banks and insurance companies routinely make meeting rooms available to community groups.

| Fund-Raising Assistance | Assigned to | Date/Time Assigned | Date/Time Completed |
|---|---|---|---|
| I. Encourage all personnel to volunteer for, participate in, and provide free, in-kind services to any non-profit organizations in headquarters plant or facility communities. Some examples are:<br>1. Annual United Fund Drive.<br>2. Hospital board and volunteer groups.<br>3. Little League teams.<br>4. Museum drives and maintenance programs.<br>5. Town (municipality) appointed boards, committees, and commissions.<br>6. Special municipal events:<br>   a. Parades.<br>   b. Celebrations.<br>   c. Festivals (annual).<br>7. Environmental groups and activities.<br>8. Service groups. | _____ | _____ | _____ |
| II. Encourage use of company auditoria, cafeterias, etc., for meetings of above groups. | _____ | _____ | _____ |
| III. Get all levels of your company employees involved with making your organization a "good neighbor" in other ways than as an employer, and as a helper in broadening the tax base. Make contact with:<br>1. Accounting personnel.<br>2. Industrial relations staff.<br>3. PR and advertising staff.<br>4. Executives at all decision-making levels.<br>5. Employees with special manual skills and expertise. | _____ | _____ | _____ |
| IV. Capitalize on these involvements and commitments; publicize employees' participation in:<br>1. House organs and company papers.<br>2. Industry publications.<br>3. Home-town papers. | _____ | _____ | _____ |

# 46

# SOCIAL REPORTING

As companies are held accountable by the public for their social performance, an increasing number are willing and sometimes eager to publish social reports. They are an extension of the financial annual report. Their aim is to report on the performance of a business from the social point of view.

The upswing in social reporting occurred in the early 70s in the heyday of student unrest and social action group activity. Exxon (then Standard Oil Company of New Jersey) published a fifty-six-page "Social Action" report, which it described as "A first report on evolving programs to meet the social responsibilities of the corporation in the world of the 1970s." Many companies have done likewise, as these examples illustrate:

- ▶ General Motors' "Public Interest Report."
- ▶ Atlantic Richfield's "Participation."
- ▶ Norton Company's "Accountability."
- ▶ Celanese Corporation's "Public Responsibility Report."

► Prudential's "Social Report."
► The American Council of Life Insurance and The Health Insurance Association of America's "Social Reporting Program of the Life and Health Insurance Business."

Most of these reports itemize and discuss those corporate actions and impacts that place a company in a favorable light. Some go further and report on what they are doing to improve their social performance in areas with negative impacts. No company is willing to completely unmask itself before the public.

Some public interest organizations are, however, attempting to penetrate corporate information walls:

► The Council on Economic Priorities (New York City) investigates corporations in several areas of social concern: environmental impact, fair employment practices, the character of political influence, and military production.
► The Interfaith Center on Corporate Responsibility (New York City) publishes a monthly newsletter, *The Corporate Examiner,* which analyzes "actions and policies of major U.S. corporations in the areas of consumerism, environment, foreign investment, policies regarding minorities and women, military production, energy, agri-business, and corporate responsibility."

These corporate accountability groups serve as an impetus for companies to do social reporting from their own viewpoint.

A social report not only has publicity value. It is a message to members of an organization that the company engages not only in the rhetoric of social responsibility but is willing to perform and be accountable in the social arena.

| Social Reporting | Assigned to | Date/Time Assigned | Date/Time Completed |
|---|---|---|---|
| I. Consider the objectives of social reports as a separate entity as well as in advertising, publicity, reports, speeches, and other company utterances: | _____ | _____ | _____ |
|   1. To enhance the company's public image in order to gain greater product acceptance, recognition of company name, and avoidance of confrontation. | | | |
|   2. To learn more about company's impact on society. | | | |
|   3. To inform society of the company's behavior and impact. | | | |
| II. Meet the following social reporting standards: | _____ | _____ | _____ |
|   1. Relevance—to need or interest in society. | | | |
|   2. Timeliness. | | | |
|   3. Significance. | | | |
|   4. Localization. | | | |
|   5. Freedom from bias—of exaggerating "good works" and playing down possible harm to society. Criteria to consider: | | | |
|     a. Fairness. | | | |
|     b. Reliability. | | | |
|     c. Verifiability. | | | |
|     d. Independent attestation. | | | |
|     e. Completeness. | | | |
|     f. Avoidance of exaggeration or puffery. | | | |
|     g. Acceptability to various audiences. | | | |
|     h. Opportunity for rebuttal. | | | |
|   6. Clarity—presented in language, format, and context understandable to different audiences. | | | |
| III. Decide on the social report's audience: | _____ | _____ | _____ |
|   1. Internal use by management only. | | | |
|   2. Shareholders. | | | |
|   3. Government officials. | | | |

*(continued)*

| Social Reporting | Assigned to | Date/Time Assigned | Date/Time Completed |
|---|---|---|---|
|     4.  Opinion leaders. | | | |
|     5.  Employees. | | | |
|     6.  Community. | | | |
|     7.  Others. | | | |
| IV.  Select format: | _____ | _____ | _____ |
|     1.  Prose only. | | | |
|     2.  Quantification. | | | |
| V.  Include the following contents. | _____ | _____ | _____ |
|     1.  Introductory information: | | | |
|        a.  Names of evaluators, their professional qualifications, relationship to the company (if any). | | | |
|        b.  Reason for undertaking evaluations, e.g., pressure from social action groups. | | | |
|        c.  Period of time during which assessment was conducted. | | | |
|     2.  Major findings, including: | | | |
|        a.  Description of social activity assessed. | | | |
|        b.  Identification of types and numbers of social impacts observed. | | | |
|        c.  Enumeration of major accomplishments and problems associated with the social activity. | | | |
|        d.  Recommendations. | | | |
|     3.  Detailed information about findings. | | | |
|     4.  Analysis of significance of findings for the company. | | | |
|     5.  Social data needs for ongoing and future monitoring of the company's activities in the audited area. | | | |
| VI.  Identify and analyze problems associated with social programs: | _____ | _____ | _____ |
|     1.  Are goals too ambitious or too modest? | | | |
|     2.  Is social performance integrated into company's regular policy review? | | | |

*(continued)*

| **Social Reporting** | **Assigned to** | **Date/Time Assigned** | **Date/Time Completed** |
|---|---|---|---|
| 3. Are social programs given too low a priority by operating management? | | | |
| 4. Are some social performance outcomes wrong or unintended? | | | |
| 5. Are your social programs changing to keep pace with your organization's changing responsibilities? | | | |

Communispond is in the business
of helping American business
communicate personally
and persuasively with its
many publics

If there's a public issue in which your
organization has a big stake, a grassroots
speaking program is worth investigating.

Such a program frequently costs less than a
routine public relations campaign. Yet it can
achieve longer-term impact on a serious
issue than a series of press releases.

For one thing, a grassroots speaking
program gets your employees involved as
on-the-scene salesmen for your viewpoint.
This not only improves morale in a basic
and lasting way, but also constitutes
effective salesmanship.

Second, a local speaking program gets
your story told — in a credible and
effective way — in the local communities
whose opinions are vital to you.

Third, since in effective local speaking
programs, speakers urge listeners to write
their Senators and Congressmen about
issues, such programs generate the kind
of letters that can influence legislators.

Last, but not least, grassroots speaking
programs involve responsible corporate
action. If a greater number of responsible
corporations take a determined stance
about getting their ideas across, it's a
good bet that American business will
prevail on such issues as Government
over-regulation.

And, today, *that's* a matter of enormous
concern to American business.

## Communispond, Inc.

*To speak as well as you think*

# How **M**obil is using a Speakers Bureau to get its ideas across at the grassroots level

One of a Series of Publications
on Management Communications by

## Communispond, Inc.

# PUBLIC
# RELATIONS
# OFFICE

The structure of the public relations office and compositions and qualifications of its personnel depend on what an organization seeks to accomplish through public relations. There is no single best organizational chart for an organization's public relations unit and its relationship to other units.

**PR AS A MANAGEMENT FUNCTION** A good starting point in planning the public relations office is to carefully examine an organization's goals and objectives:

- ► What are its leading products?
- ► What markets is it now in?
- ► What markets would it like to enter?
- ► Does it aspire to be the industry leader in sales?

By doing this, practitioners overcome a major failing that executive search firms and CEOs have pointed out: Too many public relations people don't understand the business of their employers or clients. Neither do they understand the economic system in which the company operates. To state that public relations is a management function means that every activity supports some organizational purpose.

**LINE/STAFF**  The main activities of an organization that relate to its basic mission are called "line." Activities that support the line are called "staff." The distinction becomes clear when the "output" of an organization is examined. In a manufacturing firm, products are the output. Thus, their engineering design and actual production are line functions. Personnel, purchasing, accountancy, sales, legal counsel, and public relations are staff.

Power resides in the line organization. Staff must be content with influence. The closer on the organizational chart a staff unit is to the CEO's office, the more influence it is likely to wield. Thus, public relations heads try to achieve departmental status and a reporting line directly to the CEO. The 1980 annual survey of the profession by *PR Reporter* indicates that about 55 percent of PR heads enjoy this status. Others try to gain direct access to the CEO to discuss public relations policies and important situations.

**LATERAL RELATIONS**  The ability to work well with other staff units is also important. The effectiveness of many activities and projects of public relations depend on close coordination and cooperation with others. Consider these "publics" of public relations:

▶ Employees—the personnel/industrial relations staff had chief responsibility, but employee communications is usually a public relations function.

▶ Customers—marketing/sales staff dominates, but product promotion and, to a lesser extent, consumer affairs are public relations functions.

▶ Stockholders—finance prepares financial statements; public relations is often in charge of investor communications and other financial relations.

▶ Government—lobbying and other public affairs activities are often assigned to the legal department, yet public relations is responsible for most grassroots lobbying and other public affairs communications. Monitoring of the socio-political environment may be found in either department or shared.

One of these publics is sometimes of such dominant importance to a company that public relations becomes subordinate to the staff unit representing it. In a cosmetics firm, for example, where marketing is supreme, public relations will be a unit within the marketing department.

Public relations practitioners, like other staff managers, must rely largely on persuasion to gain the cooperation of line management or lateral staffs. Having an impressive title and reporting high up on the organizational chart helps, but being regarded as expert and skillful in presenting ideas is of equal or more importance.

# 47

# HIRING PUBLIC RELATIONS STAFF

A member of a public relations staff is a generalist who knows how to apply communication skills to problems dealing with an organization's publics. Various combinations of communication and management skills, depending on organizational levels, are therefore required.

**THREE LEVELS OF PUBLIC RELATIONS** Staff positions fall on three organizational levels:

1. Executive: responsible to top management for relating public relations activities to the attainment of organizational goals. Requires a general understanding of organizational structure and behavior and specific knowledge of the employer's business. Specific responsibilities include:

Senior management counseling.

Overall supervision of public relations program.

Participation in top management policy making.

Corporate planning and strategy.

273

2. Professional:   responsible for planning and executing public relations programs. Requires seasoned judgment based on broad experience and knowledge of communication theory and human behavior. Other responsibilities include:
Budgeting.
Personnel selection and training.
Program planning and development.
Communication research.

3. Technical:   responsible for production and dissemination of public relations materials—publicity; publications to stockholders, employees, and other publics.

**WRITING**  If there is one universal qualification for a public relations position, it is the ability to write. Many organizations still insist on newspaper experience or other print media background. Slightly over half of practitioners aged forty or over held print media jobs before entering public relations, but that proportion declines with those under forty. Now, backgrounds in areas of application of public relations—marketing, advertising, and sales—appear more frequently.

**OTHER COMMUNICATION SKILLS**  On the technical level, an organization has to decide which of the following skill areas are most important to them:

- ► Newswriting and editing.
- ► Technical writing.
- ► Broadcast and communications (TV and radio production).
- ► Film writing and production.
- ► Photography.
- ► Graphic design and production.
- ► Advertising copy and layout.
- ► Public speaking.
- ► Product publicity and promotion.
- ► Media relations (also media buying).
- ► Special events.

Personality traits play a large role in public relations staffing. Honesty and integrity are important because communicators deal with society's flow of information. If that flow is corrupted, the bonds of trust that lead to common understanding are weakened. Eventually the fabric of society is destroyed.

Interpersonal communication skills are also critical: the ability to empathize—to see and feel things as others do; the ability to listen; and the ability to get along with others.

| Hiring PR Staff | Assigned to | Date/Time Assigned | Date/Time Completed |
|---|---|---|---|
| I. Once it is determined that there will be an in-house public relations department, consider the following for impact and effectiveness:<br>  1. Budget.<br>  2. Centralized or division PR account executives.<br>  3. Reporting lines.<br>  4. A table of organization for the PR department (DPR straight line reporting to) CEO and dotted line responsibilities. | _____ | _____ | _____ |
| II. Categorize personnel:<br>  1. Account executives.<br>  2. Support staff.<br>  3. Secretarial/clerical. | _____ | _____ | _____ |
| III. Account executives qualifications:<br>  1. Writing ability.<br>  2. Articulation.<br>  3. Creative ability.<br>  4. Sales ability.<br>  5. Integrity.<br>  6. Reliability.<br>  7. Aggressiveness.<br>  8. Analytical capability.<br>  9. Financial knowledge.<br>  10. Decision-making quality.<br>  11. Ability to see overall company posture.<br>  12. Ability to handle day-to-day details.<br>  13. General knowledge and frames of reference.<br>  14. Personability (getting along with others).<br>  15. Implementability (carry through).<br>  16. Potential for senior leadership post.<br>  17. Clear thinking in tense situations. | _____ | _____ | _____ |

*(continued)*

| **Hiring PR Staff** | Assigned to | Date/Time Assigned | Date/Time Completed |
|---|---|---|---|
| IV.  Staff support: | —— | —— | —— |
|    1.  Skilled in pertinent specialty. | | | |
|    2.  Writing. | | | |
|    3.  Articulation. | | | |
|    4.  Planning ability. | | | |
|    5.  Attention to detail. | | | |
|    6.  Willingness to do homework. | | | |
|    7.  Ability to carry out and interpret research. | | | |
|    8.  Willingness to be a "go-fer." | | | |
|    9.  Potential for advancement. | | | |
|  10.  Willingness to accept leadership and responsibility. | | | |
|  11.  Compatability with team workers. | | | |
|  12.  Delivers more than asked for. | | | |
|  13.  Accepts pressure gracefully. | | | |
| V.  Secretarial: | —— | —— | —— |
|    1.  Secretarial skill. | | | |
|    2.  Feeling for language. | | | |
|    3.  Anticipate needs of superiors. | | | |
|    4.  Speed in executing secretarial duties. | | | |
|    5.  Gracious personal relationship. | | | |
|    6.  Responsible. | | | |
|    7.  Ability to keep confidence. | | | |
| VI.  Clerical: | —— | —— | —— |
|    1.  Attention to detail. | | | |
|    2.  Confidentiality. | | | |
|    3.  Gracefully accepts orders. | | | |
|    4.  Necessary skills. | | | |

# 48

# CHOOSING A PUBLIC RELATIONS CONSULTANT

Situations exist when an organization requires outside public relations counseling services. First, small organizations may have no internal public relations staff. A counseling firm serves as a part-time staff to them. These clients benefit by having a far broader range of talents available to them than they would by hiring a part-time employee. Second, all organizations encounter situations when the knowledge, skills, and contacts of their own staff can benefit by being supplemented with outside counselors.

An outside counselor offers these advantages:

▶ Perspective into publics, markets, and products beyond those familiar to the client.
▶ Wider range of skills, talent, and experience which counselors obtain by working for a variety of clients and different problems.
▶ Objectivity and independence of thinking derived by not being part of the client's organization and politics.

Counseling firms vary widely according to their areas of specialization and geographic locations. The largest—Hill and Knowlton; Burson Marsteller, Ruder and Finn; and Carl Byoir and Associates—encompass most specialties and operate worldwide. They can prepare integrated, comprehensive programs dealing with consumer and environmental affairs, business and the arts, advocacy advertising, industrial publicity, grassroots lobbying, and many other specialized applications.

Regional and local firms have advantages that stem from all forms of decentralization; namely, knowledge of local conditions and media. They can also maintain frequent contact with clients located nearby.

Some firms, both large and small, offer highly specialized services that are infrequently required by clients such as:

> ► Corporate identification programs.
> ► Employee benefit communication programs.

| Choosing a Public Relations Consultant | Assigned to | Date/Time Assigned | Date/Time Completed |
|---|---|---|---|
| I. Meet or correspond, if necessary, with the managing news editors of these publications and electronic media; ask for the names of six public relations consultants who are considered to be outstanding in your area of concern:<br>　1. *Public Relations Journal.*<br>　2. *Advertising Age.*<br>　3. American Management Association.<br>　4. *Wall St. Journal.*<br>　5. *New York Times.*<br>　6. Local metropolitan dailies.<br>　7. AP and UPI.<br>　8. Local NBC, CBS, ABC, and PBS outlets.<br>　9. Your industry's official publication. | _____ | _____ | _____ |
| II. Be certain that each of these editors knows the field of concern to you:<br>　1. Financial.<br>　2. Labor.<br>　3. Product.<br>　4. Legislative.<br>　5. Scientific/Technical.<br>　6. Special fields peculiar to your company. | _____ | _____ | _____ |
| III. Assure each editor that his or her response will be held in strict confidence. | _____ | _____ | _____ |
| IV. Stress no concern for:<br>　1. Proximity to your headquarters.<br>　2. Budget size.<br>　3. Size of consulting firm. | _____ | _____ | _____ |
| V. With CEO, Executive Vice President, and Treasurer, determine need for:<br>　1. Continuous service with annual retainer.<br>　2. Spot task or "one shot" for a stated fixed fee.<br>　3. Combination of both. | _____ | _____ | _____ |

*(continued)*

| Choosing a Public Relations Consultant | Assigned to | Date/Time Assigned | Date/Time Completed |
|---|---|---|---|
| VI. Determine budget by:<br>  1. Estimating the time needed by an account executive to accomplish desired work.<br>  2. Reviewing salaries offered to PR account executives in "help wanted" ads in *Wall St. Journal,* and striking average of top figures.<br>  3. For full-time work by AE, multiply that figure by 4. This will give manpower cost.<br>  4. Add 25 percent of the total for normal expenses, travel, entertainment, photography, etc.<br>  5. If desired work will take only one-half of AE's time, multiply one-half the average salary by 4, but keep the expense figure the same as for a full-time level. | _____ | _____ | _____ |
| VII. Pick three PR counseling firms from among all the names suggested by choosing the three most common. | _____ | _____ | _____ |
| VIII. Invite each of the three firms to a pre-presentation visit.<br>  1. Ask each to prepare a pitch, allowing a decent interval of time for preparation.<br>  2. After outlining task, ask each to bring in a suggested budget, manpower needs, time needed, and costs.<br>  3. Ask for a rough idea of the approach to the recommended problem solution. | _____ | _____ | _____ |
| IX. Include in your selection committee:<br>  1. CEO.<br>  2. Executive VP.<br>  3. Operations VP.<br>  4. PR Director. | _____ | _____ | _____ |

*(continued)*

| Choosing a Public Relations Consultant | Assigned to | Date/Time Assigned | Date/Time Completed |
|---|---|---|---|
| 5. Advertising manager. | | | |
| 6. Marketing VP. | | | |
| 7. Treasurer. | | | |
| X. Following the pre-presentation meeting, ask each for personality reactions and attitudes. | _____ | _____ | _____ |
| XI. Schedule the presentations for one each day, and a day apart. Allow not more than three hours for each presentation. | _____ | _____ | _____ |
| XII. Consider the following: | _____ | _____ | _____ |
|   1. Qualifications of all those who will work on your account: | | | |
|     a. Account executives. | | | |
|     b. Account supervisor. | | | |
|     c. Implementers. | | | |
|   2. Estimated time needed to complete task. | | | |
|   3. Budget required. | | | |
|   4. Estimate of expenses. | | | |
|   5. Approach to problems. | | | |
|   6. Homework done (or its lack). | | | |
|   7. Track record of counsulting firm in allied or pertinent fields. | | | |
|   8. References. | | | |
|   9. Financial status of consulting firm. | | | |
|  10. Creativeness. | | | |
|  11. Grasp of your organization's financial, market position, and future. | | | |
|  12. Depth of knowledge of your company's products or services. | | | |
|  13. Aggressiveness. | | | |
|  14. Credibility. | | | |
| XIII. Check out references and submit copies to selection committee. | _____ | _____ | _____ |
| XIV. Allow two days for consideration and set up a meeting of the committee for a vote. | _____ | _____ | _____ |

*(continued)*

| Choosing a Public Relations Consultant | Assigned to | Date/Time Assigned | Date/Time Completed |
|---|---|---|---|
| XV. After selection, notify those who were not chosen immediately, and set up a procedural meeting with your new PR consulting firm to establish:<br>  1. Ground rules for working.<br>  2. Relationship with internal PR staff member.<br>  3. Relationship to other executives.<br>  4. Frequency of visits.<br>  5. Reporting of responsibility.<br>  6. Payment schedule for retainer, fee, and expenses.<br>  7. Demands and requirements:<br>    a. Counseling only.<br>    b. Counseling and implementation.<br>    c. Availability of other external manpower when needed.<br>  8. Definition and description of tasks.<br>  9. Limitation of authority and responsibility, internally and externally.<br>  10. Confidentiality policy. | _____ | _____ | _____ |
| XVI. Contractual factor:<br>  1. Length of contract.<br>  2. Termination terms.<br>  3. Re-negotiation.<br>  4. Renewal terms.<br>  5. Trial period:<br>    a. Long term.<br>    b. Short term. | _____ | _____ | _____ |

# **49**

# SPEECHWRITING

The value of communicating to people on an immediate, one-to-one basis has been rediscovered. CEOs and other top executives have been flocking to speaker training programs to improve their performances. The CEO knows that he or she is the organization's "communicator-in-chief." When crises occur or major policy statements are announced, the CEO's voice and words are most authoritative and credible. Other executives join in the effort to get an organization's views across to people on a personal level.

**ADVANTAGES OF** Speechmaking is one of the most potentially effective forms of communi-
**SPEECHMAKING** cation. Its specific advantages are:

> ► It is a form of personal influence which communication theo-
> rists agree is more persuasive than mass communication.
> ► It lends itself to a two-way dialogue with a live audience.
> ► It symbolizes an organization's openness and candor.
> ► It helps to "humanize" an organization.

285

**STAFFING FOR SPEECHWRITING** Few executives of Fortune 500 industrial corporations write their own speeches. They usually tell a speechwriter what to write and then seldom change the drafts. Others write their own rough draft and ask the speechwriter to edit or rewrite it. They may also take the draft written by a speechwriter and make major changes. Only about one of six CEOs write all or most of their own speeches.

Speechwriting is a specialized public relations capability. Some offices maintain full-time speechwriters; others hire them on a retainer or freelance basis. A good speechwriter is well educated and well read, knows how to string words and ideas together skillfully, and knows how to compose a speech in "spoken" rather than "written" language. Speechwriting has become one of the highest paid public relations specialties.

Writing a speech for someone else is a peculiarly personal task. A speechwriter's style and philosophical outlook must mesh with the speaker's personality. Because a speechwriter often has to talk with a wide variety of executives and specialists to gather information, he or she must be able to get along with people. Inside speechwriters are seen as top management's agent and must, therefore, remain aloof of office politics.

**USE COMMUNICATION STRATEGY** Speeches are expensive. They can cost $10,000 and more. An important cost, not to be overlooked, is the time of top managers whose time is valuable. A cost-effectiveness test must, therefore, be applied.

Every speech should be planned as if it were a communication project. These steps should always be included:

- ► Set objectives—for the entire speechmaking program as well as a specific speech.
- ► Define the audience—the "market" for the speech. Look into the inviting group's record as a speaking platform.
- ► Decide on message content—themes and material that support communication goals and are relevant to the audience.
- ► Choose the medium, your speaker, appropriate to the content and audience.

**TREAT AS NEWS EVENT** Speeches can be news events. A talk by an auto executive to blacks in Detroit or a gathering of consumerists attracts media attention. A talk is news when, for example, an oil executive speaks about the future trend of gasoline prices or replies to accusations of being profit-greedy.

Speechwriters think about their secondary audiences and ways in which newsworthy press releases can be written. They send copies of speeches and/or excerpts to magazines, particularly *Vital Speeches of the Day,* and to editors of suburban papers who are eager for materials. They ask that copies of speeches be sent to opinion leaders and others on special mailing lists.

| **Speechwriting** | **Assigned to** | **Date/Time Assigned** | **Date/Time Completed** |
|---|---|---|---|
| I. Question the need for a speech:<br>1. Substance.<br>2. Demand.<br>3. Initiative or reactive.<br>4. Specific and meaningful objective ("further the plot"). | _____ | _____ | _____ |
| II. Ascertain the delivery habits, articulativeness, capability, and philosophy of the person who will deliver the speech to be written. | _____ | _____ | _____ |
| III. Check the target audience for:<br>1. Size and composition (mixture).<br>2. Attitude (friendly or hostile).<br>3. Demand (based on need or response).<br>4. Time.<br>5. Place.<br>6. Information, promotion, or entertainment. | _____ | _____ | _____ |
| IV. Research:<br>1. Depending on audience, the depth of research should go just beyond the requirements.<br>2. Be thorough, but not to the point of boredom.<br>3. Elicit attention-getting and newsworthy material as well as background substance. | _____ | _____ | _____ |
| V. Interview the speechmaker to determine the desires and particular types of phrasing, personality, and attitude:<br>1. Conversational.<br>2. Technical.<br>3. Authoritarian.<br>4. Pedantic.<br>5. Appearance.<br>6. Delivery style. | _____ | _____ | _____ |
| VI. Set up framework by use of heads and subheads. | _____ | _____ | _____ |

*(continued)*

| | Speechwriting | Assigned to | Date/Time Assigned | Date/Time Completed |
|---|---|---|---|---|
| VII. | Flesh out and reflesh out. | _____ | _____ | _____ |
| VIII. | Read the speech outloud by yourself. | _____ | _____ | _____ |
| | 1. Rework phrases and sentences that are awkward to mouth or difficult to hear. | | | |
| | 2. Remove any place of stumbling. | | | |
| | 3. Remove redundancies and long-windedness. | | | |
| | 4. Eliminate over-folksy gambits. | | | |
| | 5. If humor or jokes are used, make them brief one-liners. Never use an individual or group as a subject of humor. | | | |
| | 6. Avoid with great care any possibility of ambiguity. | | | |
| | 7. Time the speech. | | | |
| IX. | Remember to write the speech as though it were directed at an individual. | _____ | _____ | _____ |
| X. | Allow for topical *ad libs* by the speaker. | _____ | _____ | _____ |
| | 1. Leave room for possible questions and answers. | | | |
| XI. | Time the speech and the ending which will leave the audience in an upbeat attitude or action demand. | _____ | _____ | _____ |
| XII. | Speech length is vital. Whatever time you take to recite to yourself, cut it substantially. Remember, short, significant, pithy, understandable speeches are the winners. | _____ | _____ | _____ |
| | 1. Avoid long, rambling sentences. Use simple declarative sentences. | | | |
| | 2. Generally, match the speech length with time allowed for questions and answers. Circumstances dictate the relationship; *e.g.*, highly controversial speeches with the press in attendance will require considerably more time for questions and answers than the actual length of the speeches. | | | |

*(continued)*

| | Speechwriting | Assigned to | Date/Time Assigned | Date/Time Completed |
|---|---|---|---|---|
| XIII. | Cue speaker on delivery style to begin slowly and deliberately, and then to gradually increase speed to match the acceleration in the writing.<br>1. Don't let the speaker lose the principal points.<br>2. Place in the framework of your writing, the high point at the beginning, with expatiation following—have a positive and deliberate build-up to a climax, allowing question and answer time to pick up the expatiation. | _____ | _____ | _____ |
| XIV. | If graphics, visual effects (films), models, or demonstrations are to be used, allow time and do not waste valuable points on "speech over."<br>1. Visual effects (films, graphs, etc.) must be visible from the back of the room; broad brush and substantive. Eliminate any item that does not actually add significantly to the effect of the speech.<br>2. Do not belabor the audience with obviousness. Do not have too many slides or too much film footage or too many flip charts. | _____ | _____ | _____ |
| XV. | Check out your draft with legal department, pertinent managers (stockholder relations, labor relations, etc.). | _____ | _____ | _____ |
| XVI. | Submit speech to speaker for his or her coloration:<br>1. Get him or her to substitute phrasing or "comfortable" words for your writing format.<br>2. Remember, the speech must sound as if he or she wrote it. | _____ | _____ | _____ |

*(continued)*

| **Speechwriting** | **Assigned to** | **Date/Time Assigned** | **Date/Time Completed** |
|---|---|---|---|
| XVII. If speaker is to read the speech:<br>1. Check the "prompter."<br>2. Use magnum type and non-rattling paper, allowing room on the lectern for discarded speech pages.<br>3. Be sure the timing is synchronized with his or her delivery. | _____ | _____ | _____ |
| XVIII. Have enough copies of the speech available for print and electronic news media members who are present, and also for mail releases with news style summary attached. | _____ | _____ | _____ |
| XIX. Merchandise the speech to the full extent by mailings to pertinent groups or individuals. Also mail copies with news summary to trade publications and industry headquarters. | _____ | _____ | _____ |
| XX. On occasion, an oration will be called for rather than a speech. This requires rhetorical devices such as the repetitive obvious questions that elicit audience response. This is effective more for politicians and will depend, to a great extent, on the personality of the speaker. | _____ | _____ | _____ |
| XXI. Meet these three requirements:<br>1. Have something to say.<br>2. Say it.<br>3. Sit down. | _____ | _____ | _____ |

# 50

# MAIL AND TELEPHONE HABITS

Etiquette—taste, tact, ethics, good manners—underlies mail and telephone habits. Emily Post wrote in *Etiquette,* "Truly good manners are the outward expression of an inner respect for other people. No one can fail to gain from a proper, courteous, likeable approach; or fail to be handicapped by an improper, offensive, resentful one."

How you handle telephone calls and answer letters reveals your attitude to the person on the other end. If a letter isn't answered promptly, the message is, "You're not important," or, "I have more important things to do right now." If someone places a call for you (which is an accepted practice) and you're not there when your party answers, the message is, "My time is important, but yours isn't." Discourtesy easily escalates into abusiveness.

Practical considerations should also guide mail and telephone habits. The person who placed a call or wrote a letter may need a quick response in order to make a decision or meet a deadline. A spirit of willingness to cooperate with the requirements of others is part of mail and telephone habits.

An organization's personality—its corporate image—is reflected in the appearance and style with which its letters are written. The voice of the switchboard operator or secretary answering the phone speaks for the spirit of the organization. Voice quality is as important a consideration for the selection of telephone answerers as it is for radio and television announcers.

| Mail and Telephone Habits | Assigned to | Date/Time Assigned | Date/Time Completed |
|---|---|---|---|
| Determine a corporate and divisional policy on telephone and mail habits. Write it down, have it signed by a senior executive, and send it to all staff, division, and department heads for distribution and implementation. | | | |
| MAIL | | | |
| I. Respond to all mail within twenty-four hours of receipt; acknowledgment of receipt is mandatory. | _____ | _____ | _____ |
| II. Arrange for appropriate staff, division, or department to answer requests for information pertaining to organization, service, or product. | _____ | _____ | _____ |
| III. Appoint a public relations staff person who is notably articulate, humanistic, and responsive to answer mail generally addressed to the company. Choose someone who will follow through. | _____ | _____ | _____ |
| IV. Have division or department head personally answer letters of complaint if they are addressing a specific departmental or divisional issue. Send a copy to the PR department. 1. Keep a file and log of all complaint letters. 2. Implement necessary action if required. | _____ | _____ | _____ |
| V. Answer letters from students as thoroughly as possible; don't brush them off. | _____ | _____ | _____ |
| VI. Arrange for CEO or chief fiscal officer to answer letters pertaining to the company's financial condition, stock price, changes in top personnel, mergers, acquisitions, etc. | _____ | _____ | _____ |
| VII. Provide a form letter typed out individually if the company receives numerous letters on a specific subject continually. | _____ | _____ | _____ |

*(continued)*

| Mail and Telephone Habits | Assigned to | Date/Time Assigned | Date/Time Completed |
|---|---|---|---|
| TELEPHONE | | | |
| VIII. Ask the telephone company to send in their "Telephone Habit Team." These cooperative young men and women will sit for a day or two with secretaries and telephone operators. | _____ | _____ | _____ |
| IX. Check by calling all your company numbers and assure yourself that indoctrination is being implemented and carried through. | _____ | _____ | _____ |
| X. Conduct a quick survey among 200 random persons to determine your company's image among patrons. This should be done for your own edification and that of your boss. | _____ | _____ | _____ |
| XI. Return all phone calls within a two-hour period. | _____ | _____ | _____ |
| XII. Do not allow operators and secretaries to let a caller "hang." | _____ | _____ | _____ |
| XIII. Do not allow a caller to be bucked from department to department. | _____ | _____ | _____ |
| XIV. Ask all callers their names and phone numbers if they must wait a long time. Call them immediately, or at the first opportunity. Determine whether a call is long distance. If it is, call back on your WATS line. | _____ | _____ | _____ |
| XV. Answerer should immediately give his or her name. | _____ | _____ | _____ |
| XVI. Be pleasant on the phone; the caller is not necessarily an adversary. | _____ | _____ | _____ |
| XVII. Be certain to call back if a commitment is made to return a call. | _____ | _____ | _____ |
| XVIII. Where possible, have executives make call themselves to avoid secretaries' playing the "put yours on first" game of one-upmanship. | _____ | _____ | _____ |

*(continued)*

| Mail and Telephone Habits | Assigned to | Date/Time Assigned | Date/Time Completed |
|---|---|---|---|
| XIX. Think of the attitude of the person who will be receiving your call. For example:<br>1. First thing in the morning before opening the mail.<br>2. Right after lunch when he's fussy.<br>3. Just before closing when she might be trying to catch a bus or train. | _____ | _____ | _____ |

# 51

# WAITING ROOM
# LITERATURE

A waiting room is not a place where visitors are in limbo—as if that experience were "off the record." Visitors get their first impressions of your organization when they approach the building and enter the reception area. These first impressions set the tone for everything that follows.

A waiting room serves several purposes:

- ► A resting place for visitors who have traveled.
- ► A staging area to get ready for an interview or presentation.
- ► An orientation center that tells visitors something about your organization.

Visitors are a captive audience. Their choice of what to do while waiting are mainly limited to what the reception area provides. That is why great care should go into making interesting and informative literature available. The reading option should include information about the company. Exhibits can broaden the media choice and give restless visitors who want to walk around something to do.

| **Waiting Room Literature** | **Assigned to** | **Date/Time Assigned** | **Date/Time Completed** |
|---|---|---|---|
| I. Arrange for adequate and appropriate reading material in all waiting rooms:<br>  1. General publications, *current* editions.<br>  2. Daily papers.<br>  3. Age bracket books for specific groups.<br>  4. Company publications.<br>    a. Magazines.<br>    b. Company story.<br>    c. Latest annual report.<br>    d. Product folders.<br>    e. Promotional literature.<br>  5. Prepare an 8 × 10 glossy book of unusual applications of company product. Place in an acetate folder.<br>  6. Folders of material answering visitors' possible questions about your organization. | _____ | _____ | _____ |
| II. Depending on the categories of visitors, install videotape cassettes with an adequately-sized TV set in waiting rooms.<br>  1. Although cassettes can play for as long as four hours, you can use one-hour cassettes with a relay loop.<br>  2. Select cassettes that will suit the customers:<br>    a. Cartoons for kids.<br>    b. *National Geographic* shorts for adults.<br>    c. Company or product educational shorts from exhibits or trade shows. | _____ | _____ | _____ |
| III. Display "No Smoking" sign in a prominent location—smokers should be directed to the "Smoking Area." | _____ | _____ | _____ |
| IV. Provide more individual chairs than three-seaters. Also remember an adequate coat rack must be available. | _____ | _____ | _____ |

*(continued)*

| **Waiting Room Literature** | **Assigned to** | **Date/Time Assigned** | **Date/Time Completed** |
|---|---|---|---|
| V. Arrange for the waiting room to be cleaned on a frequent and regular basis. | _____ | _____ | _____ |
| VI. Engage a receptionist with the same friendly, congenial attitude expressed by your telephone receptionist. | _____ | _____ | _____ |
| VII. Arrange for someone from the appropriate office to come out and speak to any caller who is kept waiting for a prolonged period. | _____ | _____ | _____ |
| VIII. Be certain that there are rest rooms in close proximity to the waiting room. | _____ | _____ | _____ |
| IX. Establish private "interview" rooms. Some visitors get embarrassed about stating personal facts in public. | _____ | _____ | _____ |

# **52**

# "PARISH" CALLS

The headquarters public relations office has a "functional" relationship to public relations offices on a divisional, regional, and plant level. These non-headquarters units have a direct reporting relationship to divisional and other heads, not to headquarters public relations. Yet the latter provide guidance to all public relations units throughout the organization.

Memos, packets, and phone calls epitomize what is known as the dotted line relationship. These information links are inadequate until the people on both ends of the channel get to know one another as real persons. "Parish" calls serve that purpose.

Another purpose of parish calls is to learn about local differences and problems. Centrally designed plans and policies must take these into consideration. Everything said and done during "parish" visits are taken as signals by field units as to what headquarters considers important. Care must be taken to assure that these informal cues support formal goals.

| "Parish" Calls | Assigned to | Date/Time Assigned | Date/Time Completed |
|---|---|---|---|
| I. Establish a routine of regular days for personnel to visit each division, plant, and/or department, preferably on a weekly or biweekly basis. | _____ | _____ | _____ |
| II. Designate a staff member to be responsible for each of these areas. | _____ | _____ | _____ |
| III. Set up a folder in the PR department head's office into which all agenda can be kept for discussion on your "parish" call. | _____ | _____ | _____ |
| IV. Do not preclude other timely or topical appearance by you or your staff, in addition to the mandatory regular visits. | _____ | _____ | _____ |
| V. "Parish" calls can coincide with the "vulnerability visits." | _____ | _____ | _____ |
| VI. Arrange contact list of personnel, in addition to boss, to talk to each time and see that every facet of the operation is covered. | _____ | _____ | _____ |
| VII. Look for public relations, promotional and advertising springboards, and anticipate sensitive situations. | _____ | _____ | _____ |
| VIII. Don't reject criticism and implement complaint corrections. | _____ | _____ | _____ |
| IX. Ascertain reaction of company activities in marketing, public relations, advertising, labor relations, societal activities, etc. | _____ | _____ | _____ |
| X. Familiarize yourself with personal problems of people you visit. Be interested. | _____ | _____ | _____ |

## Notes

# EXECUTIVE MEDIA EXPOSURE

With public confidence in business remaining tenuous, company executives must themselves play an active public relations role. They must "go public" and they must become the "communicators-in-chief" of their companies and industries.

Since 1973, when the Arab oil embargo thrust oil companies in the limelight, CEOs and other top managers have faced the inevitability of media exposure. They have been willing to work with public relations practitioners and other professional communicators to prepare themselves for:

    ► Television/radio appearance, panel shows, interviews.
    ► Print media interviews.
    ► Photo sessions.
    ► Government hearings as witness.

Serious weaknesses have to be recognized and overcome to develop top managers into effective public figures. Their superiority in handling hard, economic facts is often at the expense of understanding "the logic of sentiments." They tend to treat feelings and emotions as irrelevant distractions from what really counts, namely, the bottom line. They view public opinion—which is often opposed to business—as something their public relations people should change. And they equate public interest to company interest.

An executive must learn more than new media techniques when accepting a media invitation. It is an occasion to rethink the company's relationship to society. He or she must make a commitment to take a proactive stance—to speak up with the aim of producing a healthier business climate. These attitudes are unconsciously displayed in media interviews.

# 53

# TV/RADIO APPEARANCES, PANELS, AND INTERVIEWS

A growing number of business executives make television/radio appearances. They are the best representatives of their companies and American business. At a time when public confidence in business is low, their certification is essential.

The electronic media add the important personality dimensions of voice and body language to the image of business. Some experts estimate that less than 35 percent of social meaning is carried in verbal messages. The remainder is transmitted through tone of voice, gestures, posture, movement, and other nonverbal signals. People have learned rarely to trust words alone. The authenticity of verbal messages—what business credibility is all about—depends on nonverbal cues.

Some executives approach TV/radio appearances as if they were polygraph tests—as if their inner thoughts and secrets might be exposed. Although exaggerated, this apprehension is not without foundation. Experts say that interlaced fingers, a closed fist, a finger on the lips, nose rubbing, and ear pulling reveal inner conflicts. They say that clearing of the throat, closing of the eyes, scratching, and tapping the fingers or feet reveal attitudes and emotions. Raised eyebrows, meeting someone else's eyes and looking away, frowning, or smiling express doubts, likes, and dislikes, and approval and disapproval of both ideas and persons.

Radio communicates less and allows the audience to use their imaginations to fill in the total impression. But voice itself is full of meanings. A loud tone of voice may indicate anger, hostility, or alarm; a soft voice, disappointment. A raised pitch reveals tenseness, fear, or anxiety; a low pitch, calmness and relaxation. Tempo, a rasp voice, drawling, or clipping offer other cues.

Instead of pondering over all of these variables, many executives have taken a simple route. They enroll in special "telecommunication development" courses offered by leading advertising and public relations firms and by universities. Here they learn how to face a hostile newscaster, how to become aware of the above nonverbal cues, and how to know when something is said the wrong way. Sessions are taped so that executives can observe their performance in the playbacks and make necessary improvements.

Doing your homework helps.

| TV/Radio Appearances, Panels, and Interviews | Assigned to | Date/Time Assigned | Date/Time Completed |
|---|---|---|---|
| I. Prepare the executive as to subject and appearance because such appearances are generally set up in advance. | _____ | _____ | _____ |
| II. Suggest the following:<br>1. Wear a plain business suit in a medium tone—gray, brown, or blue—and a blue shirt or blouse (avoid pure white shirts for TV as they make the face appear too dark and produce a "halo" effect); men should wear a dark tie. Avoid busy patterns—stripes, plaids, checks—and highly polished jewelry that may reflect studio lights.<br>2. Ask male panelists to be freshly shaven, whether or not make-up is demanded by the producer.<br>3. Women should wear regular make-up in natural tones. Men should wear make-up if it is demanded by the producer, or if it is needed to tone down a heavy beard, shadow, or bald spot. | _____ | _____ | _____ |
| III. Eliminate personal physical mannerisms that may distract the audience. These include twisting and cracking knuckles, pulling on one's ears and nose, and wiping eye glasses, putting them on and taking them off, etc. | _____ | _____ | _____ |
| IV. Determine in advance how much ground a subject area will cover, and which topics will be presented. Executives must know their subject and be prepared to answer confidently and clearly. | _____ | _____ | _____ |

*(continued)*

| TV/Radio Appearances, Panels, and Interviews | Assigned to | Date/Time Assigned | Date/Time Completed |
|---|---|---|---|
| V. Learn the interviewer's angle and whether the interview is to be closed or open. Determine whether the interviewer seeks factual information on a specific topic or pursues a general line of questioning and depends on interviewee to develop ideas and directions. | _____ | _____ | _____ |
| VI. Set objectives to be accomplished. Prepare "mini-speeches" you can give executive to bridge into when the opportunity is right, but don't rehearse remarks until they are so pat that they sound memorized (see "Speechwriting"). | _____ | _____ | _____ |
| VII. Caution "clients"—executives who will be interviewed—to exercise extra care in making responses because of the immediacy and intractibility of the electronic news media. | _____ | _____ | _____ |
| VIII. Advise clients that it is generally better not to volunteer information during an adversary interview.<br>1. Answer completely, honestly (as far as you know), and pleasantly; avoid signs of reluctance.<br>2. Prepare the client by arranging role playing between the client and the DPR, who will act as a tough interviewer and thus enable interviewee to hammer out a proper reply and avoid being surprised. | _____ | _____ | _____ |
| IX. Don't hazard a guess. It is better to say, "I don't know" or "I can't answer that now." | _____ | _____ | _____ |
| X. Maintain an absolutely natural attitude and tone without appearing churlish or secretive. | _____ | _____ | _____ |

*(continued)*

| TV/Radio Appearances, Panels, and Interviews | Assigned to | Date/Time Assigned | Date/Time Completed |
|---|---|---|---|
| XI. Do not repeat the question each time one is asked. Answer slowly and deliberately, avoiding speech mannerisms such as "you know," or "er . . . ah." Two-second silences are not harmful; they lend an air of thoughtfulness to interviewee's responses. | _____ | _____ | _____ |
| XII. Avoid long, involved, rambling, parenthetical explanations. Simple declarative sentences are the proper response. | _____ | _____ | _____ |
| XIII. Avoid blaming others and avoid ethnic jokes. | _____ | _____ | _____ |
| XIV. Avoid throwing away what is a traumatic happening to someone else with "It's one of those things." And avoid facetiousness about serious subjects. Don't smile or grin if you're questioned about a fatal accident. | _____ | _____ | _____ |
| XV. Avoid overreaction. | _____ | _____ | _____ |
| XVI. Do not hesitate to say, "I'm sorry, I can't answer that," if the question requires a response to which you have an answer but for genuine reasons of security or jeopardy to someone else, you cannot answer it. Stick to your refusal to answer. | _____ | _____ | _____ |
| XVII. If visuals are to be used, check with TV producer or director in advance for technical compatibility. | _____ | _____ | _____ |

# 54

# PRINT MEDIA INTERVIEWS

As media interest in business and financial news rises—and it is rising—more reporters seek interviews with top executives. Newspapers and magazines want in-depth stories about a company or industry. The added human interest dimension of describing the executive enhances the story's journalistic quality.

A company benefits from media interviews by:

> ► Setting the record straight on a controversial issue affecting the company.
> ► Serving as information source for the industry or business as a whole—which enhances its corporate image.
> ► Promoting a position that relates to a company's financial marketing or public affairs objectives.

Media interviews entail risks. These are only semi-controlled situations. The executive controls what he or she says but without the luxury of time to think about surprise questions.

Public relations directors help executives by providing news releases and other information that are sent to the media. They also anticipate as many questions as possible by knowing something about the reporter's background. Some executives prefer the presence of a public relations staffer who knows both the journalist and the subject matter likely to be covered.

Public relations directors should find as many occasions as possible to role play media interviews. "What should you say to a reporter who asks . . . ?" is a game worth playing.

| **Print Media Interview** | **Assigned to** | **Date/Time Assigned** | **Date/Time Completed** |
|---|---|---|---|
| I. Most media interviews connected with company personnel will generally take place at press conferences, annual meetings, or conventions. | _____ | _____ | _____ |
| II. Emphasize to company personnel at all levels to remember that in case of the "untoward" or unpleasant happening not to:<br>1. Make assumptions without full knowledge of all facts.<br>2. Arrive at conclusion before thinking of the implications of his or her answer.<br>3. Make premature disclosure.<br>4. Violate various governmental agency or bureau requirement or prohibitions of publicly-held companies. | _____ | _____ | _____ |
| III. Although a reporter on the scene of a catastrophe (or other event) may be unhappy with a reserved response, explain to all company personnel who speak for the company to the press that it is correct procedure to say:<br>1. "I haven't all the information as yet, and cannot answer."<br>2. "It is impossible to estimate the full results of the happening—from a monetary view, so I cannot state the effect on company personnel, policies, or price/earnings" (except whether it is good or bad).<br>3. "I haven't read the whole charge, decree, or announcement (or whatever). It has legal ramifications. I'm sorry, I'll have to get back to you." Follow through. | _____ | _____ | _____ |
| IV. If the event that causes an extemporaneous interview is of major significance, point out that the interviewee must never trivialize with, | _____ | _____ | _____ |

*(continued)*

| **Print Media Interview** | **Assigned to** | **Date/Time Assigned** | **Date/Time Completed** |
|---|---|---|---|
| "Gee, it's too bad," or "This is unfortunate," or "It's just one of those things," or any statement that does not respond at the same depth as the happening. | | | |
| V. Emphasize that no company executive should ever respond with the misleading or unsatisfactory, "No comment." It is better to say, "I can't answer," or "I don't know—let me call you back." Follow through. | _____ | _____ | _____ |
| VI. Impromptu interviews are generally either inane or harmful to the company. Prevent this by preparing your executives. | _____ | _____ | _____ |
| VII. Impress on all company personnel who may be interviewed the effects on the company of their responses. | _____ | _____ | _____ |
| VIII. See "TV/Radio Appearances, Panel Shows, Interviewing Checklist." | _____ | _____ | _____ |

# 55

# PHOTO SESSIONS

No person of importance is without an official portrait or photograph. We need to visualize eminent persons or popular figures. A face gives form to a name and identity to a person. Internal communications such as annual reports and employee publications invariably print photographs of company officers and employees. They lend or confirm status and identity to those selected.

The history of business often portrays leaders of industry as villainous, ruthless, and insensitive characters who think nothing of sacrificing human welfare for private gain. Media descriptions often sound the same. A simple way to counterbalance these negative stereotypes is to replace them with photographs of real executives.

A good photograph captures the personality of an executive and humanizes the organization he or she works for. If the photograph is taken in a work setting, it says something about what the executive does.

Photos also say unintentional things. Photo after photo of company executives wearing the same dark suits and striped ties gives the impression of an authoritarian organization that demands conformity—of thought, too. Photos showing female as well as male executives, minority executives, bearded executives and other variety, depicts a different kind of organization. Collectively, photos add up to a corporate image.

| **Photo Sessions** | Assigned to | Date/Time Assigned | Date/Time Completed |
|---|---|---|---|
| I.  Do not give instructions to photographer on how to take pictures. | ——— | ——— | ——— |
| II.  Explain general purpose of desired photograph. | ——— | ——— | ——— |
|     1.  Be totally explicit about what you want. | | | |
|     2.  Purpose and use of the photograph. | | | |
|     3.  What it should and should not include. | | | |
|     4.  Desired background. | | | |
|     5.  Close up, medium shot, or long shot. | | | |
|     6.  Full figure, bust, head/hand. | | | |
|     7.  Features of products to be shot. | | | |
|     8.  Whether it should look like a studio shot or a news shot. | | | |
|     9.  It must tell the story without a caption. | | | |
|    10.  Whether it should be a provocative shot with caption explaining. | | | |
|    11.  Make the photo one that an editor can't refuse to use. | | | |
|    12.  The news medium or advertising or promotional material it will be used in. | | | |
|    13.  Color or black/white. | | | |
| III.  Let the photographer explain how he or she would like to frame the picture. | ——— | ——— | ——— |
|     1.  You explain how you see it. | | | |
|     2.  Decide before he or she starts to shoot the photograph. | | | |
| IV.  Discuss details of the session. | ——— | ——— | ——— |
|     1.  When the picture will be shot. | | | |
|     2.  Who will be available. | | | |
|     3.  Who will obtain the signatures on the photo release forms. | | | |
|     4.  Delivery date desired for proofs for editing, cropping, or enlarging. | | | |
|     5.  Date setting for finished print delivery. | | | |
|     6.  Decide who will keep negatives on file. | | | |

*(continued)*

| Photo Sessions | Assigned to | Date/Time Assigned | Date/Time Completed |
|---|---|---|---|
| 7. If no one from the PR staff will be on hand for the session, make it clear to the photographer that he or she must get clearance form signed, paying out the usual dollar fee. | | | |
| V. Emphasize to the photographer that he or she will be responsible for obtaining correct identification of all subjects and/or objects in photos. | _____ | _____ | _____ |
| VI. Let him or her know that you will write the captions. | _____ | _____ | _____ |
| VII. Arrange for rain dates or postponement dates, if necessary. | _____ | _____ | _____ |
| VIII. After proofs are chosen and edited, assign a staff member to determine and order the proper number of prints.<br>1. Assign a caption writer.<br>2. Make up distribution list.<br>3. Get a credit stamp for the back of the photos and make sure it's used.<br>4. Decide the best way for your captions to be attached to the prints and then be consistent in your format. | _____ | _____ | _____ |
| IX. Check your mailing department or mailing house to be sure proper photo stiffeners are used and proper envelopes for photos are used. Be sure that your photos are packed to arrive safely. | _____ | _____ | _____ |
| X. If photo is being shot exclusively for one publication, have the photo flagged so that there will be no inadvertent release, thus ruining your reputation with the news media. | _____ | _____ | _____ |
| XI. If company photographers are not available, arrange for reputable specialist photo stringers for use in the field or at company site. | _____ | _____ | _____ |

*(continued)*

| Photo Sessions | Assigned to | Date/Time Assigned | Date/Time Completed |
|---|---|---|---|
| 1. Assign PR staff members to work with him or her. | | | |
| 2. Local press will refer names of satisfactory photographers. | | | |
| 3. Have negatives flown back to headquarters for editing, cropping, etc., and distribution. | | | |
| XII. Devise a method of handling queries from free-lance photographers with good ideas or those on assignment. | _____ | _____ | _____ |
| 1. Allow free-lancer to shoot his or her photos and then buy them. | | | |
| 2. Don't work on a time basis with free-lancers. Decide on a mutually satisfactory fee and make sure that ownership of the negatives reverts to you. | | | |

# 56

# GOVERNMENT HEARINGS

As the federal government increasingly affects the operations and profitability of business firms, business people have learned to become active, articulate influences in the legislative process. The governmental relations or public affairs arm of public relations guides these activities.

**WASHINGTON OFFICE** Large firms typically maintain Washington offices or use law firms, public relations agencies, or other consultants to represent them. Small companies rely on their trade associations. These Washington representatives provide five services:

- ► Monitoring the Washington scene and supplying information to the home office.
- ► Lobbying.
- ► Rendering services to visiting company personnel.
- ► Providing assistance in obtaining government contracts.
- ► Supplying analyses of government programs and policies.

**CONGRESSIONAL COMMITTEES**  Congressional committees are the key to the legislative process. Bills may originate with the President, an agency of the executive branch, or the private sector: an individual, business firm, trade association, labor union, etc. All bills are referred to committees for final preparation and introduction. The interplay among the committee chairman (almost always a member of the majority party in Congress), the ranking minority members, and the professional committee staff is central to the committee system.

**LEGISLATIVE HEARINGS**  Any one of 100 Senators or 435 House members can convene a hearing. Persons for or against proposed legislation may appear, voluntarily or by order of a committee, and give testimony. Requesting time to testify at a Congressional hearing is sometimes useful. Your company establishes itself as a source of industry information. Relationships with Senators and Congressmen are thereby built.

A company's CEO can be its most effective witness. The Business Roundtable, to which CEOs of major companies belong, has learned the strategic value of chief executive testimony. But even these top business leaders can find appearing in a room with thirty-six-foot ceilings and marble walls an unnerving experience. They are unaccustomed to being asked tough questions in a fishbowl setting.

The following checklist helps to familiarize executives with the legislative process and the role that they and their public affairs representatives can play.

| **Government Hearings** | **Assigned to** | **Date/Time Assigned** | **Date/Time Completed** |
|---|---|---|---|
| I.  Assess any governmental relationship with your company, industry, or policy *via* regulation, by attending hearings and receiving information from other listening posts.<br>  1.  Develop a mutually beneficial relationship with aides of Senators from pertinent states and Congressmen from pertinent districts.<br>  2.  Visit Washington, DC, and join the National Press Club, if possible.<br>  3.  Attend a meeting of the Capitol Chapter of PRSA to be introduced to Public Information Officers (PIOs) of every potentially pertinent agency of the government, and keep these contracts active. Have copies of news releases sent to you, photo-copy them and distribute to involved company executives. | _____ | _____ | _____ |
| II.  Buy a subscription to the *Congressional Record*—it is a daily accounting of Senate and House proceedings and speeches, and statements by members of Congress.<br>  1.  Acquire a copy of the *Congressional Directory* (available from GPO) which lists all government agencies and departments, and provides data on senators and congressmen. | _____ | _____ | _____ |
| III.  Arrange for periodic visits with administrative aides (AA's) of your Senators and Congressmen, your Washington office manager, and/or legislative representative, and/or the VP in charge of such matters. Request staffs of these AA's to telephone your office in the event of any committee hearing, proposed legislation, regulatory changes, etc., that are significant to your company. | _____ | _____ | _____ |

*(continued)*

| | Government Hearings | Assigned to | Date/Time Assigned | Date/Time Completed |
|---|---|---|---|---|
| IV. | When such a notification comes, speak with the CEO and heads of appropriate departments, as well as the personnel/industrial manager to determine the effect on the company's manufacturing processes, employment, earnings, etc. | _____ | _____ | _____ |
| V. | Once the results and effects are determined, prepare a statement that includes all ammunition, no matter how slight or well known. | _____ | _____ | _____ |
| VI. | With this ammunition, arrange for your CEO to ask his or her congressional bloc for a meeting in Washington. At this time he or she will make a presentation for or against proposed governmental action. Remember that if you are in a fight, try to win with the first blow—don't nibble the opposition to death. | _____ | _____ | _____ |
| VII. | Prepare a news release embodying the company's side of the governmental action for distribution in Washington.<br>1. Be certain copies are left at hand-out table at the Press Club and at PIO offices of pertinent agencies. Be prepared for resultant press queries.<br>2. Have copies of the same materials sent from the headquarters' PR office for distribution to local media one hour before they are distributed in Washington. | _____ | _____ | _____ |
| VIII. | If the proposed government activity may result in loss of employment:<br>1. Call in union heads to a strategy meeting and prepare concomitant publicity.<br>2. Repeat above for community and industry leaders. | _____ | _____ | _____ |
| IX. | If the proposed government action could result in increased product cost: | _____ | _____ | _____ |

*(continued)*

| Government Hearings | Assigned to | Date/Time Assigned | Date/Time Completed |
|---|---|---|---|
| 1. Set up meetings among marketing, personnel, industry, and dealers/retailers for dissemination of news and to observe reactions and consequences. | | | |
| 2. Notify pertinent consumer groups for similar action. | | | |
| X. Arrange for continuing pressure until proposed activity is completed, modified, or rejected. | _____ | _____ | _____ |
| XI. If company is accused of violating some department or agency's regulations (FTC, FDA, Dept. of Justice, OSHA, etc.) meet with company general counsel, Washington legislative representative, and pertinent congressional bloc. | _____ | _____ | _____ |
| XII. If company's position is considered correct —morally, economically, or legally—mount a grassroots campaign with "truth squads" to visit pertinent locations and request that groups and individuals communicate with their Congressmen, Senators, and newspapers. | _____ | _____ | _____ |
| XIII. Explore a program undertaking advocacy advertising following a meeting of the DPR, advertising director, ad agency, and approval from the CEO. Consider whether it is appropriate for CEO to sign advertisement or to appear on TV espousing the cause. | _____ | _____ | _____ |
| XIV. Correlate all actions with required similar action by the industry. | _____ | _____ | _____ |
| XV. Consider the use of audio-visual aids, graphs, dramatic illustrations, and demonstrations of the effects of proposed or existing activity, and its effect on the community, employees, shareholders, etc. | _____ | _____ | _____ |

*(continued)*

| Government Hearings | Assigned to | Date/Time Assigned | Date/Time Completed |
|---|---|---|---|
| XVI.   Exercise extreme caution so that personal donations from corporate members are not made at a time or in a manner that might be interpreted as a contingency fee or payment. Be certain that no political donation or activity can ever be misunderstood in any way as a possible wrong doing. | _____ | _____ | _____ |

# INDEX